Dr. Rudolf Kulhanek

Improve Your English Style

Anleitung zur Aufsatzschulung und Verbesserung der mündlichen Ausdrucksweise im Englischen

14. Auflage

Neue Rechtschreibung

öbv&hpt, Wien
In Verlagsgemeinschaft mit:
Verlag Jugend & Volk, Wien
www.lisa.or.at

⚠ Kopierverbot

Wir weisen darauf hin, dass das Kopieren zum Schulgebrauch aus diesem Buch verboten ist – § 42 Absatz (3) der Urheberrechtsgesetznovelle 1996: „Die Befugnis zur Vervielfältigung zum eigenen Schulgebrauch gilt nicht für Werke, die ihrer Beschaffenheit und Bezeichnung nach zum Schul- und Unterrichtsgebrauch bestimmt sind."

Umschlagfoto: Zefa, Wien

14. Auflage, Nachdruck 2000 (14,01)

Layout und Satz: CH&ERN design, Wien
Druck: Novographic, Wien
ISBN 3-215-**01286**-3

VORWORT

Das vorliegende Nachschlage- und Übungsbuch ist eine Anleitung zur Aufsatzschulung sowie zur Verbesserung der mündlichen Ausdrucksweise im Englischen. Die aufgenommenen Mustersätze und Wendungen (patterns) sind für den englischen Stil typisch; sie kehren im geschriebenen und gesprochenen Englisch immer wieder. Ihre Kenntnis und überlegte Verwendung führen daher zu einer Ausdrucksweise, die der des Engländers oder Amerikaners sehr nahe kommt.

Der Übersichtlichkeit halber sind dem Sinn nach ähnliche Mustersätze unter zusammenfassenden deutschen Überschriften angeordnet. Weitere Bedeutungen sind in Fußnoten angegeben, um ihr rasches Auffinden zu ermöglichen.

Die links von einem Trennungsstrich angeordneten Gruppen können nach Belieben (manchmal jedoch mit verschiedenen Stilwerten) mit den rechts stehenden Gruppen verbunden werden. So ergeben sich beispielsweise für Pattern 2 insgesamt 16 Gruppen:

We live in the … age. This is the … age. Ours may be called the … age. We are on the threshold of the … age.

We live in the age of … This is the age of … Ours may be called the age of … We are on the threshold of the age of …

We live in the time of … This is the time of … Ours may be called the time of … We are on the threshold of the time of …

We live in the era of … This is the era of … Ours may be called the era of … We are on the threshold of the era of …

Mit den angegebenen Mustersätzen und Wendungen sind selbsttätig Sätze zu bilden. Zusätzlich ermöglicht ein eigener Übersetzungsteil die Überprüfung der Beherrschung dieser Phrasen an Hand von Beispielen, die die verschiedensten Lebensbereiche betreffen. Dabei ist jedem Punkt der “patterns” mindestens ein Übungssatz zugeordnet. Weitere Übungssätze betreffen die Präpositionen und Konjunktionen. Für schwierigere Wörter und Wendungen ist auf jeder Seite des Übersetzungsteiles in Fußnoten der englische Ausdruck angegeben.

Als Einleitung werden kurze Anleitungen über die Abfassung von schriftlichen Aufsätzen, Redeübungen oder Reden gegeben. Den Abschluss des Buches bildet ein Index (englischer und deutscher Teil), der das Auffinden der gewünschten Mustersätze und Wendungen erleichtern soll.

Dieses Buch wird, so hofft der Verfasser, jenen Studierenden eine Hilfe bieten, die die Schwerpunkte der englischen Grammatik bereits beherrschen. Richtig angewandt, sollte es zu einer bedeutenden Verbesserung im schriftlichen Aufsatz und in der mündlichen Rede führen.

Der Verfasser

CONTENTS

Page

Introduction 7
How Written Compositions or Talks Should Be Prepared 7
How English Debates Are Held 8

Towards Better English

Patterns (1-175) 10
Introduction and Definition 10
Reference and Example 21
Certainty or Doubt 25
Opinion or Feeling 29
General Statement and Classification 36
Time 48
Conclusion 52

Prepositions and Group Prepositions (P 1–P 89) 54

Conjunctions and Other Connectives (C 1–C 116) 60

Translation Exercises

Patterns 66
Introduction and Definition 66
Reference and Example 74
Certainty or Doubt 76
Opinion or Feeling 78
General Statement and Classification 82
Time 88
Conclusion 89

Prepositions and Group Prepositions 90

Conjunctions and Other Connectives 98

Index 105
English Part 105
German Part 112

INTRODUCTION

How Written Compositions or Talks Should Be Prepared

1. Jot down in English any ideas on the subject to be treated. Do not write the composition in German and then translate it with the aid of a dictionary.
2. Arrange the material in a logical sequence and sort it out under subheadings.
3. Arrange these subheadings, which are the topics of paragraphs, in their natural order.
4. Add an effective introduction and a suitable conclusion to provide a frame for the composition.
5. Find the best words and phrases in which this material can be expressed. Pay attention to such peculiarities of English style as the use of phrase openings, participle constructions and connectives as well as to correct tenses and word-order.
6. Imagine the reader to be quite unfamiliar with the subject you are treating. Ensure that every sentence is intelligible and says exactly what you intend to say. In short, always try to express yourself as clearly as possible.
7. When the composition has been written, read it through with the critical eye of one who is determined to find at least some of the errors that it will undoubtedly contain.

How English Debates Are Held

An English debate is a formal meeting. The chairman controls the meeting and announces the subject to be debated. The subject is called "a motion" and is worded like this: "This House considers that ..."

There are generally four main speakers. They are in two groups: two speakers support the motion and two speakers attack it. The first two are called "the proposer" and "the proposer's seconder" (speaking for the motion), and the other two are called "the opposer" and "the opposer's seconder" (speaking against the motion). The order of speaking is as follows: proposer, opposer, proposer's seconder, opposer's seconder.

After they have all spoken, the debate is "open to the floor". The floor in a debate means the audience. People in the audience may speak either for or against the motion, and when they wish to speak they must signal with their hand and await the chairman's permission. When the floor is speaking, proposers and opposers must be silent. During a speech no interruptions are allowed. When the debate of the floor is finished, summaries are given, first by the opposer, then by the proposer.

The next important stage is the voting. Every person in the House except the four main speakers has one vote, which he may use to vote for or against the motion. The votes are counted by a teller and the chairman has the casting vote (casting means deciding), if this is necessary. Members should try to cast their votes (= to vote) according to the merit of speeches and arguments which have been put forward during the debate itself rather than according to their personal feelings. The chairman then announces the result and closes the meeting.

Usually the minutes of the meeting are written down by a secretary or recorder. He must read them out at the next meeting.

What the chairman has to say in a debate

(Ladies and) Gentlemen, In our debate today the motion (= the theme) is: "This House considers (= believes) that ..."
I declare the debate opened and call upon the proposer, Mr A. –
I now call upon the opposer, Mr B. –
I call upon the proposer's seconder, Mr C. –
I call upon the opposer's seconder, Mr D. –
I now call upon the floor. –
Now we'll have the opposer's summary. –

Now we'll have the proposer's summary. –
And now the vote. How many are for? How many are against?
How many abstentions? (The House will decide by a show of hands.) –
Here is the result of the vote: ...
The motion is carried (= has been passed). Or:
The motion is defeated (= has been rejected). –
I declare the meeting closed.

Topics for a debate

Topics for a debate should be provocative; they should arouse the debaters' interest; e.g.:
This House considers (= believes) that debates should be held at school.
This House believes that Salzburg should be the capital of Austria.
This House believes that we should not spend our holidays abroad.
This House believes that a woman's place is in her home.
This House believes that Austrian football is first-rate.
The students should suggest subjects about which they would like to have a debate. They will have to prepare the debate, so that all of them can make their contributions to it.

TOWARDS BETTER ENGLISH

PATTERNS

INTRODUCTION AND DEFINITION

1 Sehr geehrter Herr Vorsitzender! Meine Damen und Herren! Es ist eine große Freude (und Auszeichnung) für mich, (bei dieser Tagung) zu Ihnen sprechen zu dürfen.

Mr. Chairman, Ladies and Gentlemen,	
It is a great pleasure (and privilege) It is an honour	for me to speak to you. for me to address this meeting. for me to introduce …
First of all, On behalf of … (and myself)	I should like to welcome … I should like to extend a warm welcome to …

2 Wir leben im Zeitalter des …

We live in This is Ours may be called We are on the threshold of	the … age. the age of … the time of … the era of …

---

1 eine Ehre, … vorzustellen; Zunächst (Im Namen … und im eigenen Namen) möchte ich … begrüßen,… herzlich willkommen heißen
2 Wir stehen an der Schwelle

3 sind überzeugt; behaupten; sind der Meinung; interessieren sich für; schätzen; denken kaum an; könnten sich nicht vorstellen
5 Es gibt Anzeichen dafür, dass …
6 es wurden bedeutende Verbesserungen erzielt, Anstrengungen unternommen; es hat größere Veränderungen gegeben; es wurden ausgezeichnete Ergebnisse erzielt; es fand eine rasche Entwicklung statt

3 Viele Leute glauben, dass …

There are many people who Most of us More and more people	(tend to) think that … (find it difficult to) believe that … are convinced that … maintain that … are of the opinion that … are interested in … have come to know and enjoy … give little thought to … could not imagine …

4 Wir könnten uns … nicht mehr aus dem Leben wegdenken.

We could not imagine It is almost impossible to imagine	(modern) life without …
(Modern) Life would be unimaginable without …	

5 Heutzutage neigt man zu …

Nowadays At present	there is a tendency there is a trend	towards (noun) … to (verb) …
	there are indications that …	

6 In letzter Zeit wurden bei … bedeutende Fortschritte erzielt.

Lately Recently In recent years It is only recent- ly that In the past few decades During the last few months Over the past few years	rapid progress has been made in … striking advances have been achieved in … notable improvements have been achieved in … (considerable) efforts have been made to … important successes have been achieved in … major changes have occurred in … excellent results have been obtained in … there have been rapid developments in the field(s) of …

7 Interessante Versuche werden derzeit angestellt, um …

Interesting experiments are now being made Important experiments are being carried out Investigations into … are being undertaken Research into … is being conducted	(in order) to … in (the field of) … on a large scale. on a considerable scale.

8 Man kann … als … definieren.

… may be … has been … can best be	defined as … described as … called … termed …

9 … war der Erste (der Einzige), der … behandelte.

… was the first … was among the first … was the only one	to deal with … to show … to reveal … to disclose … to prove … to demonstrate … to describe … to recognise … to solve …

10 … nimmt eine hervorragende Stellung unter … ein.

… holds … has maintained	a prominent a predominant a leading an outstanding	position place	among(st) … in …
… is outstanding … is leading … ranks high			

7 Forschungen, die sich mit … beschäftigen, werden (in großem Maße) betrieben.
9 … gehörte zu den Ersten, die behandelten; enthüllten; bewiesen; beschrieben; erkannten; lösten
10 … hat eine führende Stellung behauptet

11 … gehört (zählt) zu den größten …

<table>
<tr><td colspan="2">… is among
… ranks among
… is perhaps</td><td rowspan="2">the greatest …
the finest …
the most famous …
the most outstanding …
the most notable …
the most important …
the most essential …
the most representative …
the most characteristic …
the most typical …
the most influential …
the most popular …
the most modern …
the most up-to-date …
the most versatile …</td></tr>
<tr><td>… is considered to be
… is reputed to be
… is believed to be
… is regarded as
… is looked upon as
… is known as
… is renowned as
… is appreciated as
… is esteemed as</td><td>(one of)</td></tr>
</table>

12 … stellt einen großen Fortschritt auf dem Gebiete des … dar.

<table>
<tr><td>… constitutes</td><td>a considerable advance
a remarkable improvement (over)
a valuable innovation
a(n) historic step</td><td>in (the field of) …</td></tr>
</table>

13 … ist einer der berühmtesten Orte des Landes.

<table>
<tr><td>… is one of the country's</td><td>most renowned
most famous
most popular
best known
most frequently visited</td><td>places.
cities.
spas.
watering-places.
(holiday) resorts.
beauty spots.
sights.
recreational areas.</td></tr>
</table>

---

11 schönsten; hervorragendsten; bemerkenswertesten; wesentlichsten; einflussreichsten; beliebtesten; vielseitigsten

12 … stellt eine bemerkenswerte Verbesserung (gegenüber …), eine wertvolle Neuerung, einen historischen Schritt dar

13 gehört zu den beliebtesten, bekanntesten, meistbesuchten Heilbädern, Kurorten, Urlaubsorten, Naturschönheiten, Sehenswürdigkeiten, Erholungsgebieten

14 … liegt in …

… is located … is situated … lies	in … on … off … amid … midway between …

15 … ist eines der bemerkenswertesten … Zentren (Veranstaltungen).

… is one of … is among	the most remarkable the most important the most outstanding the greatest the best known	scientific cultural literary artistic music(al) religious scholastic sporting economic industrial political social	centres in … events

16 … ist ein Meilenstein (Wahrzeichen).

… is	a landmark a turning-point a corner-stone one of the highlights of … a great achievement an engineering (a technological) feat an ingenious method of …

14 an, auf; auf der Höhe von, gegenüber; inmitten; genau zwischen
15 wissenschaftlich; künstlerisch; Schul-; Sport-; wirtschaftlich; gesellschaftlich
16 Wendepunkt; Grundstein; Höhepunkt; großartige Leistung, Errungenschaft; technische Großtat; geniale Methode

17 … ist eine Vorrichtung, die zu … dient.

… is	a device an appliance an apparatus an instrument a kitchen utensil a domestic appliance a household gadget a machine a system an installation	which serves for … which serves many purposes. which is intended for … which is designed for … which proves of inestimable value. which is extensively used in … (for …) which is commonly employed in … which is largely applied in … which is being adopted in … whose use is widespread. whose application is universal.

18 Es gibt verschiedene Mittel (Arten) …

There are	various several numerous	means of … ways of … methods processes sorts kinds types varieties classes groups

19 Unsere Kenntnisse über … beruhen auf …

Our knowledge of … … is an invention which	is based (mainly) upon … is founded on … is centred upon … depends (largely) upon … rests upon … is due to …
We owe our knowledge of … to …	

17 ein Gerät, das vielen Zwecken dient; ein für … bestimmter Apparat; ein für … bestimmtes Instrument; ein Küchengerät, das sich als überaus wertvoll erweist; ein Haushaltsgerät; eine Maschine, die (in …) viel verwendet wird; eine Anlage, deren Verwendung weit verbreitet ist

18 process = Verfahren

19 … ist eine Erfindung, die … ; Wir verdanken … unsere Kenntnis(se) über …

20 Heutzutage ist fast jeder mit … vertraut

Nowadays nearly everybody is	familiar with … conversant with … acquainted with …
It is common knowledge that …	

21 … ist untrennbar mit … verbunden.

… is	inseparably associated with … closely connected with … intimately linked (up) with … bound up with … in close connection with … in close association with …

22 … besteht (hauptsächlich) aus …

… consists of …		
… is	basically principally chiefly mainly largely essentially primarily	made up of … composed of …

23 … spielt (nach wie vor) bei … eine wichtige Rolle.

… plays … continues to play	an important an essential a major a leading an active a vital a paramount	part in … role in …

---

20 Es ist allgemein bekannt, dass …
21 … hängt eng mit … zusammen

24 … wird von Jahr zu Jahr (bei …) beliebter.

<table>
<tr><td>… is gaining more and more</td><td>popularity
favour
ground</td><td rowspan="2">(among …)
(with …)</td><td rowspan="3">every year.</td></tr>
<tr><td colspan="2">… is becoming more and more popular</td></tr>
<tr><td colspan="3">… is coming more and more into the forefront</td></tr>
</table>

25 Die Bedeutung des … wird heute (in letzter Zeit) voll erkannt.

The importance of … The necessity of … The need for …	is being fully realised nowadays. has been fully realised lately. cannot be overstressed.

26 Wenn man … (richtig) beurteilen will, muss man etwas von … wissen.

If we want to appreciate … (fully), In order to judge … correctly, To understand …	we must have some idea of … we should know something about … we should remember that … we must bear in mind that … we must familiarise ourselves with … we should be conversant with … we must become acquainted with …

27 Aus Zeitungsberichten ist zu entnehmen, dass …

From reports and statements in newspapers (and magazines)	we gather that … we learn that …

---

25 British English: mostly -ise, -iser, -isation (e.g.: organise, organiser, organisation); American English: -ize, -izer, -ization (e.g.: organize, organizer, organization); kann man nicht genug unterstreichen
26 sollte man nicht vergessen, dass …; muss man bedenken, dass …; muss man sich mit … vertraut machen; sollte man mit … vertraut (werden)

28 Es war eines der seltsamsten ..., die sich jemals ereigneten.

It was one of	the strangest … the queerest … the most extraordinary … the most unusual … the most remarkable … the most memorable … the most exciting … the most thrilling … the most amazing … the most astounding … the most captivating … the most fascinating … the most decisive … the most daring …	that ever happened. I ever read (about). I ever witnessed. I ever came across. I ever heard (of).

29 Zunächst (in diesem Zusammenhang) möchte ich … behandeln.

First of all, To begin with, To start with, At the beginning, At the (very) outset (In this connection) (In this context)	I should like to I am going to let me	deal with … describe … define … explain … point out … mention … give you an idea of … draw your attention to …
	let us consider … let us recall … let me remind you of …	

30 Zunächst, was versteht man unter …?

First of all, what do we mean by … ?

28 eines der sonderbarsten, ungewöhnlichsten, bemerkenswertesten, denkwürdigsten, aufregendsten, spannendsten, verblüffendsten, fesselndsten, bezauberndsten, entscheidendsten, kühnsten …, denen ich jemals beiwohnte, die ich jemals antraf, die ich jemals hörte

29 ich möchte beschreiben, definieren, darauf hinweisen, erwähnen, Ihnen eine Vorstellung von … geben, Ihre Aufmerksamkeit auf … lenken; wir wollen berücksichtigen = beachten; uns ins Gedächtnis zurückrufen; ich darf Sie daran erinnern

31 Bevor wir auf … eingehen können, müssen einige Punkte berücksichtigt werden.

Before we can embark on …,	a number of factors must be	considered. borne in mind. taken into account. taken into consideration.
	it is important to realise …	
Before approaching the subject from the viewpoint of … Before discussing … Before going into details	we should	be aware of … be conscious of … remember … bear in mind …

32 In diesem Aufsatz (Vortrag) will ich einen kurzen Überblick über … geben.

In this composition In this talk In this lecture	I am going to give a brief I should like to give a brief	survey of … account of … description of … summary of …
	I shall concern myself (primarily) with … I should like to discuss …	

33 Das Thema des … ist …

The subject of … The topic of … The (central) theme of …	is …

31 Bevor wir an das Thema vom Standpunkt des … herangehen können, bevor wir … besprechen können, auf Einzelheiten eingehen können, ist es wichtig, … zu erkennen, sollten wir uns … bewusst sein, sollten wir … nicht vergessen, sollten wir … bedenken

32 talk = Vortrag, Redeübung – Bericht, Beschreibung, Kurzfassung; ich will mich (in erster Linie) mit … beschäftigen; möchte ich über … sprechen

33 theme: also of music; topic: mostly of a talk, lecture or speech

34 Der Hauptzweck des … ist … (Der einzige Zweck des … ist …)

The primary The sole The only	object aim purpose task function	of … is …

35 Das Buch behandelt (in erster Linie) …

The book The volume The magazine The brochure The article	(in question)	deals (primarily) with … is about … contains … roughly covers the period from … to … covers a wide field thoroughly.
The contents of … are The (under)plot of the play is The argument is		as follows: …

36 Ein altes Sprichwort sagt, dass …

There is an old	saying proverb belief legend	(that …)
An old adage The story	goes that …	
Tradition has it that …		

37 Jahrhundertelang (Früher) nahm man an, dass …

For (many) centuries Formerly In former times	it was	assumed taken for granted argued	that …

34 task = Aufgabe
35 Der Band, die Zeitschrift, die Broschüre handelt von, enthält, behandelt in großen Zügen die Zeit von … bis … ; behandelt ein umfangreiches Gebiet gründlich; der Inhalt, die (Neben)Handlung des Stückes, der Hauptinhalt ist wie folgt: …
36 belief = Glaube
37 behauptete man

Reference and Example

38 Wie unten (oben) erwähnt,...

As will be This will be As (was)	mentioned explained stated indicated pointed out referred to dealt with described shown demonstrated proved seen	below, later, (above), (before), (earlier), (previously),

39 Hier möchte ich ... (nicht) behandeln.

Here I am (not)	referring to ... concerned with ... dealing with ...

40 Übrigens vergaß ich.... zu erwähnen.

By the way, I forgot to mention ...

41 Ich möchte noch etwas erwähnen: ...

There is another thing I should like	to mention: ... to deal with: ... to say: ... to refer to: ...

42 Man kann noch hinzufügen, dass ...

It may (also) be added that	
A (further) note A remark	may be added on ...

---

38 festgestellt; angegeben; ausgeführt; hingewiesen; behandelt; beschrieben; erörtert; bewiesen

43 Es bleibt jedoch noch ein weiteres Problem: ...

There remains yet a further problem: … It now remains for me to explain …

44 Wir wollen uns jetzt ... zuwenden.

<table>
<tr><td rowspan="2">(Now)</td><td>Let us</td><td>turn to
examine
come back to</td><td rowspan="2">(a question
we previously
left aside.)</td></tr>
<tr><td colspan="2">Let me draw your attention to</td></tr>
</table>

45 Ich möchte nun einige Beispiele anführen.

<table>
<tr><td>(Now)</td><td>Let me give
Let us turn to
Let us consider</td><td rowspan="2">some examples.
another example.
a few examples
illustrating …</td></tr>
<tr><td colspan="2">As a proof … of let me cite
Here are (Here is)</td></tr>
<tr><td colspan="3">Let us take the example of …</td></tr>
</table>

46 Aber ich will nicht zu lange bei diesem Thema bleiben.

However, I do not wish to dwell upon this subject too long. I shall, however, refrain from dwelling on this subject too long. I will, however, drop this subject now. Going into details would carry me too far.

47 Hier sind einige Höhepunkte seines Lebens: ...

Here are some of	the highlights the main features	of his life: … of his career: …

---

43 Es bleibt mir nur noch übrig zu erklären ...
44 Kommen wir nun zu einer Frage zurück, die wir vorher beiseite ließen. Ich möchte nun Ihre Aufmerksamkeit auf ... lenken.
45 Als Beweis für ... möchte ich nun einige Beispiele anführen, die ... beleuchten.
46 Ich möchte jedoch dieses Thema jetzt fallen lassen. Es würde zu weit führen, wenn wir uns über Einzelheiten ausließen.
47 Grundzüge

48 Als Beispiel möchte ich … erwähnen.

As an example By way of example As an instance For instance, For example, Above all, Among other things, By comparison,	let me I should like to	mention … cite … quote … refer you to …

49 Man kann einige Beispiele (Gründe) für … anführen.

A few examples of … A number of reasons for …	can be given.
Let us illustrate this by looking at several examples.	

50 Es gibt viele derartige Beispiele (Fälle).

There are many such	examples. instances.

51 Natürlich gibt es Ausnahmen; aber sie sind so selten, dass man sie nicht in Betracht zu ziehen braucht.

Of course, there are exceptions; but they are so rare that they may be disregarded.

52 Dieses Beispiel ist eine Ausnahme, die die Regel bestätigt.

This example is This example furnishes	an exception which proves the rule. an exception to the general rule.

53 Ich habe mich auf diese wenigen Beispiele beschränkt, weil …

I have	restricted myself to confined myself to concentrated on	these few examples these few remarks	because …

---

48 Zum Beispiel, vor allem, unter anderem, vergleichsweise möchte ich anführen (cite), zitieren (quote), Sie auf … verweisen.

54 All das betrifft ...*)

All this	relates to ... concerns ... refers to ...

55 Wie der Name (Titel) schon sagt, ...

As the name As the title	implies, ... suggests, ...
As denoted by the heading, ...	

*) was ... betrifft, was ... anlangt = as to; as regards; with (= in) regard to; with (in) respect to

CERTAINTY OR DOUBT

56 Ich bin (ganz) sicher, dass ...

I am I feel	(absolutely) certain that ... (almost) sure that ... (quite) positive that ... (fully) convinced that ... (fully) aware that ... inclined to agree with many others that ...

57 Ich weiß aus meiner eigenen Erfahrung, dass ...

From my own experience From past experience	I know that ...
I know perfectly well that ...	

58 Es ist klar, dass ...

It is	obvious evident apparent	that ...
It seems only natural It is hardly surprising		

59 Offenbar (Wahrscheinlich) ...

Obviously,... Evidently, ... Apparently, ... Presumably, ... Probably, ... In all probability, ...

---

56 überzeugt, bewusst, ich stimme mit vielen anderen darin überein, dass ...
57 Ich weiß sehr wohl, dass ...
58 Es scheint nur zu natürlich, dass ...; es überrascht kaum, dass ...
59 presumably = vermutlich; in all probability = aller Wahrscheinlichkeit nach

60 Es ist sehr (un)wahrscheinlich, dass …

It is It appears It seems This makes it appear	(highly) probable (very) likely (most) improbable (rather) unlikely	that …

61 Das ist besonders bei … der Fall.

This is	particularly so particularly evident	in the case of …

62 Man kann nicht leugnen, dass …

It cannot be denied It must be admitted It goes without saying It stands to reason It scarcely need be said I need hardly tell you It is scarcely necessary to point out	that …

63 Es besteht kein (kaum ein) Zweifel darüber, dass …

There is	no doubt no denying no need to point out little doubt	that …

64 Zweifellos …

Doubtless, … No doubt, … Undoubtedly, … Without doubt, … Beyond doubt, …

---

62 Man muss zugeben, dass …; es versteht sich von selbst, dass …; es ist kaum nötig zu sagen, dass …

65 Es ist zweifelhaft, ob …

It is	doubtful unknown uncertain	whether …
There is some uncertainty		

66 Tatsächlich …

Actually, … As a matter of fact, … In fact, … The fact is that … It is a fact that …

67 Ich möchte wissen, ob …

I wonder I should like to know We do not (yet) know (for certain)	if … whether … (or …) when, what, which, why, (from) where, which way, who, whose, whom, how …

68 Auf den ersten Blick könnte man meinen, dass …; aber nach genauerer Überprüfung wird man sicherlich finden, dass …

At first sight At first glance At first perusal	we might believe that …; it appears that …; it seems that …; one tends to believe that …;	but
on a closer view on more careful inspection on closer examination on closer consideration on reflection on second thoughts after careful study if we look more closely, if we go to the root of the matter,	we shall certainly find that … it comes to this: … the following becomes clear: …	

---

65 unbekannt; ungewiss
66 actually = eigentlich, tatsächlich; note: aktuell = topical, current
68 perusal [pə'ru:zl] = Durchsicht; on reflection, on second thoughts = bei genauerer Überlegung; if we go to the root of the matter = wenn man der Sache auf den Grund geht

69 Jedenfalls (Auf alle Fälle) ...

In any case, … In any event, … At any rate, … At all events, … By all means, … Anyway, …

70 Keinesfalls (Auf keinen Fall) ...

On no account, … In no case … By no means …

70 followed by inversion of subject and verb!

Opinion or Feeling

71 Nach meiner Meinung …

In my opinion, …
In my view, …
To my mind, …
For my taste, …
As for myself, …
I, for my part, …
I feel that …

72 Ich bin der Meinung, dass …

I am of the opinion that …
I am under the impression that …
I have a feeling that …
It seems to me that …

73 Ich nehme an, dass … (Vermutlich …)

I presume I suppose I expect	that …

74 Nach … zu schließen, kann man annehmen, dass …

Judging from … Judging by …	we may assume we may conclude we may suppose	that …

75 … soll (angeblich) …

… is said to …
… is considered to …
… is supposed to …
… is presumed to …
… is expected to …
… is believed to …

72 Ich habe den Eindruck, das Gefühl, dass …; es scheint mir, dass …

76 Ich muss zugeben, dass ...

I must admit I am (not) prepared to admit It must be confessed I do not dispute	that …

77 Ich kann nicht umhin zu denken, dass ...

I cannot help I cannot resist	thinking feeling mentioning stating adding	that …
I cannot but think		

78 Ob Sie es glauben oder nicht, ...

Believe it or not, … Strange as it may seem, … Anyway, I am persuaded of its truth.

79 Es ist (nicht) schwer, sich vorzustellen, dass ...

It is (not) difficult I find it difficult I find it hard	to imagine that … to believe that …
Frankly, I do not believe … I do not hesitate to believe …	

---

76 Ich bin (nicht) bereit zuzugeben, dass …; man muss gestehen, dass …; ich bestreite nicht, dass …

77 Ich kann nicht umhin zu glauben, zu erwähnen, festzustellen, hinzuzufügen

78 So seltsam es auch scheinen mag, … Jedenfalls bin ich davon überzeugt, dass es wahr ist.

79 Ich finde es schwer zu glauben, dass …; offen gesagt, ich glaube es nicht; ich zögere keinen Augenblick zu glauben …

80 Das gilt (auch) für ...

This holds true for ... The same holds for ... This is (equally) true of ... This applies to ...

81 Was für ... gilt, muss auch für ... gelten.

What is true of ... must necessarily be true of ..., too. What applies to ... will certainly apply to ... as well.

82 In Wirklichkeit (Gott sei Dank) trifft (genau) das Gegenteil zu.

In fact, As a matter of fact, Actually, Thank heavens,	the contrary the converse precisely the opposite	is true.

83 Obwohl es ziemlich unglaubwürdig klingt, ist es doch wahr.

Though this Although this	sounds seems	rather incredible, rather strange,	it is perfectly true.
Incredible as this may seem,			

84 Das ist ... zuzuschreiben.

This is	(probably) (largely) (particularly) (partly)	due to ... because of ...

85 Das erklärt ...

This explains ... This accounts for (the fact that) ... This may account for ... This supplies the key to (this problem).

84 (wahrscheinlich, hauptsächlich, besonders, teilweise)

86 Das ist einfach eine Frage des …

This is	simply (and solely) purely merely only exclusively mainly largely predominantly primarily rather	a question of … a matter of …

87 Hier erhebt sich die Frage, ob …

Here the questions arises This raises the question This raises the point Controversy exists as to	whether …

88 Das beweist, dass …

This proves This is a proof	that …

89 Das ist mit … unvereinbar.

This is	incompatible inconsistent irreconcilable	with …

90 Vieles spricht für (gegen) …

There is a great deal to be said	for … in favour of … against …

---

86 rein; bloß; nur; ausschließlich; hauptsächlich; weitgehend; besonders; in erster Linie; eher

87 Es bestehen Meinungsverschiedenheiten darüber, ob …

91 Es ist von größter Wichtigkeit, dass ...

It is	of the greatest significance of the utmost importance (most) important essential	that ... for us to ...
What *does* matter is that ...		

92 Es ist ja nicht sehr wesentlich, ob ...

After all, it does not matter (very much) It matters little	whether ...

93 Es ist für ... unbedingt nötig.

It is	absolutely necessary indispensable	for ...

94 Man sollte ... nicht vernachlässigen (unterschätzen, überschätzen).

We should not It would be a (bad) mistake to	neglect ... ignore ... overlook ... underrate ... underestimate ... undervalue ... exaggerate ... overrate ... overestimate ... overvalue ... attach excessive importance to ... attach too much significance to ...

---

91 essential = wesentlich
94 nicht beachten; übersehen; unterbewerten; übertreiben; überbewerten; übermäßige (zu große) Bedeutung beimessen

95 Man sollte (mehr) Wert auf … legen.

(Greater) (More) (Due) (Special)	Attention should be paid to … Consideration should be given to … Emphasis (Stress) should be laid on … Care should be taken when …

96 Das wird (muss, kann) zu … führen.

This	will (inevitably) must need not cannot may (eventually)	result in … lead to … bring about … cause … create … give rise to …

97 Es mag sein, dass, …

It may well be that … It is true that … It sometimes seems as if …

98 Es wäre (für …) unmöglich (zwecklos) zu …

It would be	impossible useless	(for …) to …

99 Gott sei Dank (Glücklicherweise) …

I am	happy glad pleased delighted	to say that …
Fortunately, … Luckily, … Thank heavens, …		

---

95 Man sollte … größere Aufmerksamkeit zollen, mehr berücksichtigen, genügend betonen, besondere Sorgfalt walten lassen

96 eventually = schließlich, endlich; note: eventuell = possibly, perhaps

100 Leider (Unglücklicherweise) …

I am sorry to say that … Unfortunately, …

101 Es ist schade, dass …

<table>
<tr><td colspan="2">What a pity
It can only be regretted</td><td rowspan="2">that …</td></tr>
<tr><td>It is
It has always seemed to me</td><td>(most) unfortunate
(most) regrettable
a pity</td></tr>
</table>

---

101 Es ist bedauerlich, dass …; man kann nur bedauern, dass …

General Statement and Classification

102 Genau genommen …

Strictly speaking, … Generally speaking, … Broadly speaking, … Comparatively speaking, … Historically speaking, …	
In general, Roughly, Broadly,	(we may say that …)

103 Im ursprünglichen Sinn bezeichnet es …

In its	original literal figurative	sense use meaning	it denotes it means	(nothing more than) … (the same as) …
In a general				
Literally, Figuratively,				

104 Das möchte ich … nennen.

This is	what I (would) call … what is called … the so-called …
In a sense, it may be called …	

105 Es ist sozusagen …

It is,	so to speak, as it were, …

106 Kurz, …

Briefly, … To be brief, … In short, … In a word, … To put it in a nutshell, …

107 Mit anderen Worten

In other words, … To put it differently (and perhaps more accurately), … That is to say, …

108 Unter diesen (allen, keinen) Umständen …

In Under	the (best) any no *	circumstances …

109 Unter bestimmten Bedingungen …

Under	certain such the most favourable	conditions

110 Für diesen besonderen Zweck …

For this particular	purpose … circumstance …

111 Bei dieser Gelegenheit …

On	this (that) one another a similar	occasion

112 In diesem Falle …

In that case, … In such cases, …

---

102 Im Allgemeinen; im weitesten Sinn; vergleichsweise; historisch betrachtet
103 Im wörtlichen (übertragenen) Sinn

* followed by inversion of subject and verb!
107 Um es anders (und vielleicht genauer) auszudrücken, das heißt
109 Unter den günstigsten Bedingungen
111 Bei einer ähnlichen Gelegenheit

113 In mancher Hinsicht …

In many In some In several	ways, … respects, …
From certain points of view, …	

114 Im Notfall

In an emergency, … If the worst comes to the worst, …

115 in einem bestimmten Grad …

To	a certain some the same a much greater a most remarkable an ever-increasing a lesser such a(n)	degree, … extent, …

116 Wie es häufig der Fall ist, …

As is	frequently the case, … customary, … usual, …
As frequently happens, …	
As might be expected, …	

117 Das heißt nicht, dass … (es heißt nur, dass …)

This is not to say that … (it is only to say that …) This does not mean that … (it only means that …)

118 Dasselbe kann man von … sagen.

The same A few words	may be said of … might be said about …

---

115 In gewissem, in bemerkenswertem, in zunehmendem, in geringerem Maße
116 Wie es üblich ist, … Wie zu erwarten ist, …

119 Es ist bemerkenswert, dass ...

It is	noteworthy interesting to note important to remember worth considering worth mentioning worth remembering	that ...
What is important to realise is What I am most interested in is		

120 Es ist überraschend, dass ...

It is	surprising astonishing startling amazing almost incredible almost unbelievable	that ...
The surprising thing is What is particularly striking is What I am greatly surprised at is		
Surprisingly enough, ...		

121 Das ist für ... typisch.

This is	typical characteristic peculiar	of ...

122 Es zeichnet sich durch ... aus.

It is characterised by ...

---

119 Es ist interessant festzustellen; es ist wichtig, daran zu denken, erwägenswert; erwähnenswert; erinnerungswürdig; es ist wichtig, sich darüber im Klaren zu sein; am meisten interessiert mich

120 erstaunlich; Aufsehen erregend; verblüffend; fast unglaublich (unglaubwürdig); besonders auffallend; am meisten bin ich darüber überrascht, dass ...

123 Das beeinflusst …

This	influences … affects … bears on … determines … impairs … exerts a considerable influence on …
This has a	considerable effect on … a great impact on … a direct bearing on …

124 Das erleichtert …

This	facilitates … simplifies … improves … necessitates … enables … ensures …
This makes …	easier. simpler. worse. (un)necessary. (im)possible.

125 Das erhöht …

This	increases … adds to … raises … favours … promotes … furthers … enhances … accelerates … permits … allows …

---

123 Das wirkt sich auf … aus; wirkt auf … ein; bestimmt; beeinträchtigt; übt einen großen Einfluss auf … aus; hat auf … eine große Wirkung (Einwirkung), eine direkte Auswirkung
124 Das vereinfacht, verbessert, macht notwendig, ermöglicht, gewährleistet
125 Das vergrößert, steigert, begünstigt, fördert, erhöht, beschleunigt, gestattet, erlaubt …

126 Das vermindert ...

This	decreases … reduces … prevents … eliminates … avoids …

127 Das geschieht, um ... (nicht) zu steigern.

This is being done	with a view to for the purpose of with the object of with the aim of	increasing … reducing … eliminating …
	in order to so as (not) to	increase … reduce … eliminate …

128 Das hat zu ... geführt.

This This urgent need	(has*)	resulted in … led to … brought about … caused … induced …
	gave (has given*)	rise to … birth to …

129 ... hat sehr zu ... beigetragen.

… (has*)	greatly importantly considerably	contributed to(wards) …	
	made	outstanding important valuable pre-eminent	contributions to(wards) …
… did (has done*) much to …			

* up to now
126 Das setzt herab, verhindert, beseitigt, vermeidet ...
127 um (nicht) zu vermindern, beseitigen
128 Das hat ... verursacht, veranlasst
129 ... hat zu ... einen hervorragenden (wichtigen, wertvollen) Beitrag geleistet

130 Das wird sich als (überaus) wertvoll erweisen.

This will	prove be	(most) (particularly) (extremely)	valuable. beneficial. useful.

131 ... ist unübertroffen.

... is	unsurpassed unparalleled unrivalled unmatched unequalled without equal	
Nothing can	match ... compare with ...	
There is nothing like ...		
It compares	(un)favourably easily	with ...

132 Es entspricht den Erfordernissen (des ...).

It meets It copes with	(all) the requirements the needs the exigencies the expectations the increasing demand the growing demand	of ...
It comes up to expectations.		

---

130 (besonders) zuträglich; (höchst) nützlich
131 Es schneidet (un)günstig gegenüber ... ab; es nimmt es mit ... leicht auf
132 Es deckt den steigenden Bedarf an ...; es entspricht den Erwartungen; exigency = dringender Bedarf

133 … wird (auf diesem und verwandten Gebieten) viel verwendet.

… is	extensively widely largely universally frequently successfully	used employed utilised adopted applied exploited	(in this field and its related fields.) (in this and other fields.)
	in wide use. widespread.		

134 Diese Methode wurde eingeführt (wird verwendet).

This method This technique This process	has been	introduced adopted applied employed used discarded	(in …)

135 Es gibt mehrere wesentliche Unterschiede (Ähnlichkeiten).

There are several	essential important fundamental striking	differences similarities

---

133 Also: … is used extensively, etc. – weitgehend; allgemein; häufig; to exploit = ausnützen, ausbeuten
134 technique (tek'ni:k) = method; cp. engineering (science) process = Verfahren; to discard = aufgeben, verwerfen
135 grundlegend; auffallend

136 Es entspricht …

<table>
<tr><td colspan="3">It corresponds to …
It closely resembles …
It is directly proportional to …</td></tr>
<tr><td rowspan="2">It is</td><td>exactly
much
about
roughly</td><td>the same as …</td></tr>
<tr><td colspan="2">identical with …
equal to …
similar to …</td></tr>
</table>

137 Es ist (ganz) anders als …

<table>
<tr><td>It is</td><td colspan="2">(quite) different from …
in sharp contrast to …</td></tr>
<tr><td colspan="3">It makes a brilliant contrast against …</td></tr>
<tr><td>It differs</td><td>widely
considerably</td><td>from …</td></tr>
<tr><td>It contrasts</td><td>sharply
in a marked way</td><td>with …</td></tr>
<tr><td colspan="3">It is inversely proportional to …</td></tr>
</table>

138 Wir wollen (können) zwischen … unterscheiden.

<table>
<tr><td rowspan="2">Let us
We may
We are apt to
It is possible to</td><td>differentiate
distinguish
make a distinction</td><td>between … and …</td></tr>
<tr><td colspan="2">contrast … and …</td></tr>
</table>

---

136 Es ähnelt … sehr; ist zu … direkt proportional; ist genau, ungefähr dasselbe wie …

137 Es steht zu … im scharfen Gegensatz; bildet zu … einen prächtigen Kontrast; unterscheidet sich von … stark (beträchtlich); hebt sich deutlich von … ab; ist zu … verkehrt proportional

139 Man kann sie wie folgt einteilen: …

<table>
<tr><td>They may be</td><td>classified
classed
arranged
grouped
graded
summed up</td><td colspan="2">as follows: …
in various ways.
in a variety of ways.
under the following heads: …
under such headings as …</td></tr>
<tr><td>They may be</td><td>(sub)divided
further divided</td><td rowspan="2">into the following
into various</td><td rowspan="2">classes.
categories.
groups.
divisions.</td></tr>
<tr><td colspan="2">They fall</td></tr>
</table>

140 Dazu gehört (gehören) …

It includes … It comprises … It covers …

141 Wie alles andere hat es sowohl Vorteile als auch Nachteile.

<table>
<tr><td colspan="2">Like everything else, it has both advantages and disadvantages.
First of all, let us consider its advantages.</td></tr>
<tr><td rowspan="2">Here are
Let me mention</td><td>some of the chief advantages that this type possesses (offers).</td></tr>
<tr><td>some of the disadvantages (drawbacks, limitations) that this type has (suffers from).</td></tr>
</table>

---

139 auf verschiedene Weise, unter verschiedene Titel, in verschiedene Klassen, Kategorien, Gruppen ordnen, zusammenfassen, unterteilen

141 Wir wollen zunächst seine Vorteile betrachten. Hier sind einige Hauptvorteile, die diese Type besitzt (bietet). Ich will einige Nachteile (Schattenseiten) erwähnen, die diese Type hat (unter denen sie leidet).

142 Verschiedene Schwierigkeiten treten auf.

Various difficulties Similar problems	arise are met with are encountered must be faced must be dealt with must be approached must be tackled
Certain difficulties must be overcome. These problems must be solved.	

143 Wir müssen ... loswerden.

We must get rid of …

144 Alle diese Hilfsmittel sind heute vorhanden.

All these facilities are now	available. provided (for). at our disposal.

145 ... zeigt sich in seinen Werken

… is	shown revealed mirrored reflected	in his	works masterpieces descriptions

146 Das beweist seine Vorliebe für ...

This Much in his work	proves reveals shows mirrors	his predilection for … his preference for … his taste for … his love of … his dislike of …

142 Auf ähnliche Probleme stößt man; man sieht sich ihnen gegenüber; muss an sie herangehen; muss ihnen begegnen; muss sich mit ihnen beschäftigen; muss mit ihnen fertig werden. Bestimmte Schwierigkeiten muss man überwinden. Diese Probleme müssen gelöst werden.
144 Sie stehen uns zur Verfügung.
145 ... spiegelt sich in seinen Meisterwerken (Beschreibungen)
146 Vieles in seinem Werk zeigt (spiegelt wider) seine Neigung für; Liebe zu; Abneigung gegen ...

147 Dass er ein Meister des … war, kann man aus … ersehen.

That he was a master of … can be seen from …	
How great his art was can be seen	by comparing his works with … by contrasting his works and …

148 Seine Größe (als …) liegt in …

His greatness as … His genius	lies in …
It is for … that his name is best remembered.	

147 Man kann die Größe seiner Kunst erkennen, wenn man seine Werke mit … vergleicht.
148 Durch … ist sein Name am meisten bekannt.

149 Am Anfang (Ende, an der Wende) des … Jahrhunderts …

At About Towards Shortly after Just before Not before Since Until By	the beginning of the end of the close of the turn of	the … century …
In the middle of Early (Late) in		
By mid-century …		

150 (Erst) Als diese Periode zu Ende ging (begann), …

As When Not before *	that period that era the century that decade	came to an end (began), … drew to a close, … closed (opened), …

151 Es geht in (das Jahr) … zurück.

It dates from It dates back to It goes as far back as It extends back to It does not go back further than It has been traced as far back as	the … century. 1666.

* followed by inversion of subject and verb

149 ungefähr; gegen; kurz nach; knapp vor; erst; seit; bis; in der Mitte des … Jahrhunderts

150 dieses Zeitalter; Jahrhundert; Jahrzehnt

152 Im beginnenden (auslaufenden) … Jahrhundert …

In the	early (late) … century … latter part of that century … late 18th and early 19th centuries … late 1950's and early 1960's …
In late 1966 and early 1967 … From the 16th to the 18th centuries …	

153 In der unmittelbaren Nachkriegszeit …

In the immediate	post-war period … pre-war years …
Between	the two world wars … the first and second world wars … World War I and World War II …

154 Heutzutage (Gegenwärtig) …

Nowadays … In the current century … At present …

155 Früher …

Previously … Formerly … In former times … In the past … In ancient times … In his time … In Chaucer's days … In the reign of …

---

152 Im zweiten Teil dieses Jahrhunderts; im auslaufenden 18. und beginnenden 19. Jahrhundert; in den späten fünfziger Jahren und den frühen sechziger Jahren; Ende 1966 und Anfang 1967; vom 16. bis zum 18. Jahrhundert
153 In den Jahren unmittelbar vor dem Krieg; zwischen den beiden Weltkriegen
155 In früheren Zeiten; in der Vergangenheit; in alten Zeiten; während der Regierung …

156 Neulich (unlängst, neulich am Morgen, neulich am Abend) …

Recently …
The other day …
Not too long ago …
A week (A fortnight) ago …*
The other morning …
The other night …

157 Gleichzeitig …

Simultaneously …
At the same time …

158 Inzwischen …

Meanwhile …
In the meantime …

159 Von Zeit zu Zeit …

At intervals …
From time to time …
Every now and then …

160 Im (gegenwärtigen) Augenblick, derzeit …

For the time being …
At the moment …
At present …

161 Im Laufe der Zeit …

In the course of time …
As time went on …
In the long run …

* Opposites: today week = heute in einer Woche; today fortnight = heute in 14 Tagen

156 Vor einer Woche (Vor 14 Tagen)

162 Zuerst – dann – schließlich

At first …	Then … (Shortly) Afterwards … After a while … Later (on) … Subsequently …	At last … In the end … Finally … Eventually … At length … Ultimately … In the long run …
First of all …		Last of all …

163 Bis jetzt …

Up to Till Until	now …
So far …	

164 Damals …

Then … At that time …

165 Vor dieser Zeit …

Before that time … Before then … Previously …

164 then = da, dann, damals; note: the then president

CONCLUSION

166 Zusammenfassend (abschließend) kann man sagen, dass ...

Summing up Summarising	we may say that (under existing conditions) …
In concluding, In closing, In conclusion, In the end, To summarise, To sum up,	it may be said that … let me say that we can only hope that … let me point out that there are indications of … it might be well to remember … it may be well to repeat once more that … let me emphasise once again: … let me repeat (emphatically): …

167 Alles in allem glaube ich, kann man sagen, dass ...

On the whole, All in all, All things considered,	I believe that it is correct to say that … I think (it would be best to) … I (do not) think that eventually … I feel that … it is to be expected that … it seems safe to say that …

168 Wenn man die Vor- und Nachteile berücksichtigt, kann man schließen, dass ...

Considering (all) its advantages and drawbacks, After weighing the pros and cons,	we may conclude that … we may arrive at (come to, get to) the conclusion that … we may reach the conclusion that …

169 So haben wir gesehen, dass ...

Thus we have seen Thus it is The conclusion is	that …

---

166 (unter den gegenwärtigen Verhältnissen); wir können nur hoffen, dass …; ich möchte darauf hinweisen, dass Anzeichen für … vorhanden sind; es ist gut, sich an Folgendes zu erinnern; es wäre vielleicht gut, nochmals zu wiederholen; ich möchte nochmals betonen; ich möchte (mit Nachdruck) wiederholen

167 ich glaube, es wäre am besten, zu …; ich glaube (nicht), dass schließlich …; ich denke, dass …; es ist zu erwarten, dass …; man kann mit gewisser Sicherheit sagen, dass …

169 So kommt es, dass … ; die Schlussfolgerung ist, dass …

170 Aus den angegebenen Gründen ...

It is for the reasons stated that ...

171 In diesem Aufsatz (Vortrag) habe ich mich bemüht zu beweisen, dass ...

In this composition (In this talk) I have endeavoured to prove that ...

172 Was immer die Zukunft bringen mag, man kann erwarten, dass ...

Whatever the future may hold, Whatever may happen in the future, Be it as it may, We do not know what lies in store for us in the future, but Although the outcome is unpredictable,	it may be expected that ... it is to be hoped that ... one thing is certain: ... there is (every) reason to believe that ...
Looking further ahead we may expect that ...	

173 Nur so wird es möglich sein, ... zu ...

Only in this way Only by this means	will it be possible to ... may we accomplish the task of ...

174 Zollen wir daher jenen Anerkennung, die ...

Let us, therefore, offer We should, therefore, pay	tribute to those who ...

175 Das mag eine Möglichkeit für die (nahe – ferne) Zukunft sein.

This may well be a possibility for the (near – distant) future.

---

172 Wie immer dem auch sei, es ist zu hoffen, dass ...; wir wissen nicht, was uns die Zukunft bringt, aber eines ist sicher: ...; obwohl das Ergebnis nicht vorherzusagen ist, besteht (jeder) Grund zur Annahme, dass ...; wenn man einen Blick in die Zukunft tut, kann man erwarten, dass ...

173 Nur so können wir die Aufgabe erfüllen.

PREPOSITIONS AND GROUP PREPOSITIONS*

P 1	abgesehen von	apart from; except for
P 2	an	at; against on; upon (a river)
P 3	angesichts	in view of; considering
P 4	anstatt	instead of; in place of
P 5	auf	on; upon; at the top of; on (the) top of; on to = onto; up to (direction)
P 6	auf Grund von	on account of; on the strength of; on the grounds of; by reason of; due to
P 7	auf der Höhe von	off (Dover)
P 8	aus	from; out of; made of
P 9	aus … heraus	(from) out of; from within
P 10	außer	besides; in addition to; over and above ("plus") except (for); but; save; with the exception of; excepting; excluding; barring** ("minus")
P 11	außerhalb	outside; out of
P 12	bei	at; by; near (place) with (persons and general terms) in (general terms)
P 13	bereits (in)	as early as; as long ago as; as far back as; already in

* In alphabetical order. – For further uses, prepositions are to be studied together with the words governing them; e.g.: interest in; arrive at; wait for; depend on; etc.

** barring holidays

P 14	binnen	within
P 15	bis	to (place and time) as far as (place) till = until (time: ununterbrochen bis) by (time: bis spätestens) (right) up to; down to
P 16	bis auf	to within (distance) except; but; with the exception of (excluding)
P 17	bis nach	as far as (place) till after = until after (time)
P 18	dank	thanks to; owing to
P 19	diesseits	on this side of
P 20	durch	through by (passive voice)
P 21	durch ganz	throughout; all over (Europe)
P 22	einschließlich	including
P 23	erst (nach)	not before; not till; not until; not till after; as late as
P 24	für	for; in favour of; in exchange for; for the sake of (um … willen)
P 25	gegen	towards; in the direction of (direction) against (opposition) by (time) versus; vs.; v. (sport, jurisdiction)
P 26	gegenüber	opposite; facing (place) as against; compared with (comparison) (advantage) over
P 27	gemäß	according to; in accordance with pursuant to; in pursuance of (jurisdiction)
P 28	gleich nach	immediately after (time and place) on; upon; shortly after (time)

P 29	hinauf auf	up (to) on to; onto
P 30	hinsichtlich	as to; as for; concerning; regarding; respecting; relating to; referring to; with (= in) regard to; with (= in) reference to; with (= in) respect to; as regards … ; inasmuch as … is concerned; as far as it is connected with …; in matters of; in point of; from the point of view of; from the standpoint of
P 31	hinter	behind; at the back of beyond (the mountains)
P 32	hinter … hervor	from behind
P 33	hinunter zu (nach)	down (to)
P 34	im Falle des	in (the) case of; in the event of
P 35	im Gegensatz zu	contrary to; in contrast to; as contrasted with; unlike; in opposition to
P 36	im Namen von	on behalf of
P 37	im Vergleich zu	(as) compared with; in comparison with
P 38	im Verhältnis zu	in proportion to
P 39	im Zusammenhang mit	in connection with; in connexion with
P 40	in	in; at (rest) into; to (motion) inside; within
P 41	in Anbetracht des	considering; in consideration of; in view of
P 42	in Bezug auf	relating to; relative to; with regard to; in regard to; as regards; as to
P 43	in der (nächsten) Nähe des	near (by); close to; close by; adjoining; next to; in close proximity to
P 44	infolge	in consequence of; owing to; due to; as a result of

P 45	in ganz	throughout; all over (Europe)
P 46	inmitten	amid(st); in the midst of; in the middle of
P 47	innerhalb	within; inside
P 48	in Übereinstimmung mit	in accordance with; in conformity with; in agreement with; in compliance with
P 49	in Zusammenarbeit mit	in co-operation with; in collaboration with
P 50	je nach	according to; depending on
P 51	jenseits	beyond; on the other side of
P 52	knapp vor	just before; immediately before
P 53	kraft	by (= in) virtue of
P 54	längs	along
P 55	laut	according to as per (commerce)
P 56	mangels	for want of; for lack of; failing*
P 57	mit (zusammen mit)	with (along with; together with; associated with; in association with; in conjunction with) by (car, train, etc.)
P 58	mittels	by means of; with the help of; with the aid of
P 59	nach	after; … later (time) to; as far as (place) according to; in accordance with (gemäß)
P 60	namens	on behalf of
P 61	neben	beside; by the side of
P 62	oberhalb	above
P 63	ohne	without; but for; if it were not for; if it had not been for**

* failing which = widrigenfalls; for lack of evidence = mangels an Beweisen

** e.g.: I could not do it if it were not for your help (= without your help). – I could not have done it if it had not been for your help.

P 64	ohne Rücksicht auf	regardless of; irrespective of
P 65	seit	since (point of time) for (period of time)
P 66	seitens	on the part of
P 67	statt	instead of; in place of
P 68	teils durch … teils durch	what with … and*
P 69	trotz	in spite of; despite; notwithstanding
P 70	über	over; above (place) across (quer über) by way of; via (a town or a country) about; of (information) on (a topic)
P 71	über … hinaus	beyond
P 72	um (etwa um)	at; (about; at about)
P 73	um … (herum)	round; around; about; round about; all round; on every side of
P 74	um … willen	for the sake of
P 75	ungeachtet	irrespective of; regardless of; notwithstanding
P 76	unten an	at the bottom of
P 77	unter(halb)	under; below; beneath; underneath (place) among; from among (group)
P 78	unter … hervor	from under
P 79	von	from (direction, time)** of (= about) by (passive voice) out of; in (a number)***

* e.g.: What with the terrible heat and the effect of the long ascent, we felt awfully tired.

** Note: as from January 1st = vom 1. Jänner an

*** e.g.: five out of ten – five in ten

P 80	von … weg	off; away from
P 81	vor	in front of; ahead of; before (place) … ago; before; prior to (time) with (after adjectives: red with, etc.)
P 82	vorbei an	past
P 83	… vorher (früher)	… before; … earlier; … previously
P 84	während	during; for pending (jurisdiction)
P 85	wegen	because of; owing to; on account of; for; as a result of; by reason of; due to
P 86	wider	contrary to; against
P 87	wie	like*
P 88	zu	to (motion) at; in (rest) in addition to; over and above; besides ("plus") for (purpose)
P 89	zwischen	between **

* Note: "like" (wie) – "as" (als): He works like a scientist. He works as a scientist.
** in between = dazwischen

CONJUNCTIONS AND OTHER CONNECTIVES*

C 1	aber	but; however
C 2	allerdings	it is true
C 3	als	when (time) as (während) than (comparison)
C 4	also	consequently; therefore; that is why; hence
C 5	als ob	as if; as though
C 6	andernfalls	otherwise; else; or else
C 7	angenommen	supposing (that); assuming (that)
C 8	auch	also; too; likewise
C 9	auch … nicht	not … either nor (+ inversion of subject and verb) neither (+ inversion of subject and verb)
C 10	außer dass	except that; save that
C 11	außer (wenn)	unless
C 12	außerdem	in addition; besides; moreover; furthermore; apart from that
C 13	bevor	before
C 14	beziehungsweise	and … respectively; or … respectively**
C 15	bis	until; till

* In alphabetical order. Note: In subordinate temporal and conditional clauses (clauses beginning with "after", "as long as", "before", "till", "until", "when", "whenever", "if", "in case", "unless") the future time is generally shown by either the present tense or the present perfect tense. Examples: He will finish his work before he goes. – He will go out as soon as he has finished. – She will come unless it rains.

** e.g.: in the north-west and north-east of London respectively

C 16	da	there (place) then (time) as; since (= because)
C 17	da doch, da nun	since; now that
C 18	daher	so; that is why; hence; therefore; as a result; the result is that; for that reason; that is the reason why; on that account; owing to this fact; on account of this fact
C 19	damit	so that; in order that; in such a way that
C 20	damit nicht	so that … not; in order that … not; lest; for fear that*
C 21	dann	then; from that time on(wards); after that time – (außerdem) in addition; besides; moreover; furthermore
C 22	das heißt	i.e.**; that is to say; that is; that means
C 23	dass	that
C 24	demgemäß	accordingly
C 25	denn	for
C 26	dennoch	(and) yet; notwithstanding; nevertheless; nonetheless; in spite of that; despite all that; all the same; for all that; even so; however
C 27	deshalb	so; therefore; that is why
C 28	dessen ungeachtet	notwithstanding
C 29	doch	yet; however; nevertheless
C 30	ebenfalls	likewise; also; too; … as well
C 31	ebenso … wie	as … as
C 32	ehe	before

* e.g.: We worked carefully, lest we should make mistakes. – We remained silent, for fear that they should hear us.

** Latin: id est = that is

C 33	einerseits … andererseits	on the one hand … on the other (hand)
C 34	entweder … oder	either … or
C 35	erst wenn; erst als	not … until; not … till; not before; only after … (followed by inversion of subject and verb)
C 36	falls	in case; if
C 37	ferner	in addition; furthermore; moreover; besides; apart from that
C 38	folglich	consequently; as a consequence; in consequence
C 39	freilich	admittedly, though
C 40	genauso wie	just as; exactly as
C 41	gleichfalls	likewise; … as well; also; too
C 42	gleichsam	as it were; so to speak
C 43	hernach, hierauf	then; after that time; from that time on(wards); afterwards
C 44	im Gegenteil	on the contrary
C 45	immer wenn	whenever; as often as
C 46	insofern	inasmuch as; in so far as
C 47	je … desto	the … the
C 48	jedoch	…, however, …; though*
C 49	je nachdem, ob	according as
C 50	jetzt da, nun da	now that
C 51	kaum … (da)	no sooner** … than; hardly** … when; scarcely** … when
C 52	nachdem	after; when

* e.g. : three months later, however; three months later, though, …

** followed by inversion of subject and verb

C 53	nämlich	viz*; namely; to wit
C 54	natürlich	of course
C 55	nicht einmal	not even
C 56	nicht so … wie	not so … as; not as … as
C 57	nicht nur … sondern auch	not only … but (also)
C 58	nichtsdestoweniger	nevertheless; nonetheless
C 59	noch; noch immer	still
C 60	noch immer nicht	still not
C 61	noch nie	never before*
C 62	noch nicht	not yet
C 63	nur; nur mehr	only
C 64	ob	if; whether
C 65	obgleich, obwohl	though; although; in spite of the fact that
C 66	oder	or
C 67	seit (dem)	since; ever since
C 68	seither	since that time; ever since
C 69	selbst wenn	even if; even though; even when
C 70	so	thus; in this way
C 71	sobald (als)	as soon as
C 72	sobald einmal	once**
C 73	sodass	so that; in order that; in such a way that
C 74	sofern	provided (that)
C 75	sogar	even
C 76	solange (als)	as long as; so long as

* Latin: videlicet – namely

** e.g.: once this has happened; once this has taken place; once this has been done; once this has been achieved

C 77	sondern	but
C 78	sonst	else; or else; otherwise
C 79	sooft (als)	as often as; whenever
C 80	so … wie	as … as
C 81	sowie	as well as
C 82	sowohl … als auch	both … and
C 83	sozusagen	so to speak; as it were; in a manner of speaking
C 84	teils … teils	partly … partly
C 85	trotzdem	all the same; (and) yet; in spite of that; despite all that; notwithstanding; for all that; even so; even so, however; nevertheless; nonetheless
C 86	überdies	moreover; besides; in addition
C 87	übrigens	by the way
C 88	um nicht zu	so as not to; in order not to
C 89	um zu	to; so as to; in order to; with a view to*
C 90	und	and
C 91	ungeachtet, ob …, oder …; gleichgültig ob … oder	no matter whether … or …
C 92	unter der Bedingung, dass	on condition that
C 93	vielmehr	rather
C 94	vor allem	above all
C 95	vorausgesetzt, dass	provided (that); providing (that)
C 96	während	while; whilst; as whereas (contrast)

* with a view to + -ing; e.g.: with a view to improving

C 97	wann (auch) immer	whenever; whensoever
C 98	was	what which (= and that)
C 99	was (auch) immer	whatever; whatsoever
C 100	weder … noch	neither … nor
C 101	weil	because
C 102	weiterhin	furthermore
C 103	wen (auch) immer	whomsoever
C 104	wenn	when (time) if (condition)
C 105	wenn auch	even if; even though
C 106	wenn nicht	unless; if … not
C 107	wer (auch) immer	whoever; whosoever
C 108	wie	as (explanation) how (indirect question) such as (examples)
C 109	wo	where
C 110	wogegen	whereas
C 111	woher	from where; where … from
C 112	wohin	which way; where … (to)
C 113	wo(hin) immer	wherever
C 114	worauf	whereupon; on (= upon) which; after which
C 115	zum Beispiel	e.g.*; for instance; for example; such as
C 116	zwar	it is true; indeed

* Latin: exempli gratia = for instance

TRANSLATION EXERCISES

PATTERNS*

INTRODUCTION AND DEFINITION

1 Sehr geehrter Herr Vorsitzender! Meine Damen und Herren! Es ist eine große Freude und Auszeichnung für mich, bei dieser Tagung zu Ihnen sprechen zu dürfen. -
Zunächst möchte ich Sie herzlich begrüßen.

2 Wir leben in einer Zeit rascher Fortschritte und gewaltiger Veränderungen. Unsere Zeit kann man sowohl das Zeitalter des Autos als auch das Atomzeitalter nennen.

3 Immer mehr Menschen sind der Meinung, dass ein weiterer großer Krieg von verheerenden Folgen für die Menschheit wäre. Manche neigen sogar zur Annahme, dass im Falle eines weltweiten Krieges der ganze Erdball zerstört werden würde. –
Es gibt viele Menschen, die einen Urlaubsaufenthalt an einem ruhigen Ort, fern von den Urlaubermassen, schätzen. –
Die meisten Leute, die anfangen, eine Fremdsprache zu lernen, denken wenig an die großen Anstrengungen, die nötig sind, um eine angemessene praktische Kenntnis dieser Sprache zu erwerben.

4 Heutzutage könnte man sich die modernen Massenmedien nicht mehr aus dem Leben wegdenken. –
Es wäre schwer, sich ein Leben ohne Elektrizität vorzustellen. Es wäre auch fast unmöglich, sich aus dem heutigen Leben die modernen Maschinen wegzudenken, die unsere Arbeit erleichtern und beschleunigen.

5 Heute herrscht eine starke Tendenz zur Erzeugung von Produkten aus Kunststoff oder Kunstfasern. –
In unseren Tagen gibt es Anzeichen dafür, dass in naher Zukunft Prob-

---

* Numbers refer to the patterns (1 — 175).

1 meeting

3 to be of disastrous consequences for; a world-wide war; globe; a holiday stay; holiday crowds; a fair working knowledge of a language

4 to facilitate; to accelerate

5 plastic; artificial (man-made) fibre (A.: fiber); not too long ago; unsolvable

leme gelöst werden können, die vor nicht allzu langer Zeit als unlösbar betrachtet wurden.

6 In letzter Zeit sind bedeutende Fortschritte auf fast allen Gebieten des menschlichen Lebens erzielt worden. –
Während der letzten Jahre hat es größere soziale Veränderungen in vielen Ländern der Welt gegeben. Erst in jüngster Zeit sind beträchtliche Anstrengungen unternommen worden, um möglichst vielen Menschen eine gründliche Schulbildung zu bieten. –
In den letzten Jahrzehnten sind ausgezeichnete Ergebnisse in der medizinischen Forschung und auf verwandten Gebieten erzielt worden.

7 Gegenwärtig werden interessante Versuche angestellt, billigere Treibstoffe herzustellen. –
Derzeit werden in großem Maße Forschungen betrieben, die sich mit den wirksamsten Lehr- und Lernmethoden beschäftigen. –
Wichtige Experimente werden derzeit auf dem Gebiete der Technologie angestellt.

8 Das Adverb kann als Wortart definiert werden, die ein Zeitwort, ein Eigenschaftswort oder ein anderes Umstandswort näher bestimmt. –
Man hat Geoffrey Chaucer, den Verfasser der berühmten Canterbury Tales, den Vater und Begründer der englischen Dichtkunst genannt. –
Edinburgh, das oft „das moderne Athen" genannt worden ist, wird von vielen Leuten mit Salzburg verglichen.

9 Sir James Maxwell war der Erste, der die Existenz der Radiowellen nachwies. –
Lord Rutherford, ein in England arbeitender Neuseeländer, war der Erste, der bewies, dass das Atom einen Atomkern haben müsse. Er war auch der Erste, der einen Wasserstoffkern erhielt, indem er einen Stickstoffkern mit Alphateilchen bombardierte.–
Zwei Amerikaner waren die ersten Menschen, die den Mond betraten. –
Ein kleines Kind war der einzige Passagier, der das furchtbare Unglück überlebte.

10 Salzburg nimmt unter den Festspielstädten der Weit eine hervorragende Stellung ein. –

---

6 thorough education (= schooling); related fields
7 to provide fuels; efficient
8 a word; to modify; Geoffry ['dʒefrɪ], Edinburgh ['edɪnbrə]; Athens [æ]
9 a nucleus – some nuclei [ɪaɪ] hydrogen [aɪ]; nitrogen [aɪ]; alpha particles; to bombard; to set foot upon; to survive
10 tourist traffic, tourist trade, tourist industry, tourism; to hold a rowing contest

Der Südwesten Englands hat seine führende Stellung im britischen Fremdenverkehr gehalten. –
Der Ruderwettbewerb zwischen den Universitätsmannschaften von Oxford und Cambridge, der jedes Jahr auf der Themse durchgeführt wird, nimmt eine hervorragende Stellung im englischen Universitätssport ein.

11 Der Tower, die Tower Bridge, die Westminster Abbey, das Parlamentsgebäude mit dem Big Ben, die St. Pauls Kathedrale, der Hydepark, der Trafalgar Square mit der Nelsonsäule sowie der Piccadilly Circus mit der Erosstatue zählen zu den beliebtesten Londoner Sehenswürdigkeiten. –
Scarborough ist vielleicht der schönste und berühmteste Badeort an der englischen Ostküste. Torquay hingegen ist als einer der beliebtesten Urlaubsorte in Devon bekannt. –
Genauigkeit, Arbeitsersparnis, Klarheit und Zweckmäßigkeit werden als wesentlichste Kriterien für eine gute Buchhaltung angesehen. –
Das Rad wird als eine der bemerkenswertesten Erfindungen in der Geschichte der Menschheit betrachtet. –
Das österreichische LD-Verfahren wird in vielen Ländern der Welt als eine überaus wirtschaftliche Stahlerzeugungsmethode geschätzt. Es stellt eine bemerkenswerte Verbesserung gegenüber den früheren Stahlerzeugungsmethoden dar.* –
Man glaubt, dass diese Anlagen zu den modernsten in Europa zählen. –
Sir Walter Scott, der Verfasser einer ganzen Reihe hervorragender historischer Romane, gilt als einer der einflussreichsten Schriftsteller des 19. Jahrhunderts. –
Mozart wird von vielen als der bedeutendste österreichische Komponist angesehen. –
Das Penicillin wird als eines der bedeutendsten Heilmittel geschätzt. –
Sir Winston Churchill gehörte zu den vielseitigsten Menschen seiner Zeit. Er war nicht nur Soldat, Politiker und Staatsmann; er war auch ein bekannter Maler und Schriftsteller.

12 Die Unterzeichnung der Magna Charta durch König Johann im Jahre 1215 stellt ein bedeutendes Ereignis in der englischen Geschichte dar. Sie legte die Grundlage zur britischen Verfassung.

13 Strafford-upon-Avon ist eine der berühmtesten und am häufigsten besuchten Städte Englands. –

---

* See also Pattern 12.

11 seaside resort; accuracy; economy of labour; utility; factor; steel-making method; remedy

12 to lay the foundation of

Die Niagarafälle gehören zu den bekanntesten Naturschönheiten Nordamerikas. –
Badgastein, einer der beliebtesten Kurorte, ist ein bedeutendes Wintersportzentrum. –
Der Lake District in Nordwestengland gehört zu den meistbesuchten Erholungsgebieten in Großbritannien.

14 Die Vereinigten Staaten sind (Singular!) ein Land, das genau zwischen der Zone tropischer Hitze und der Zone arktischer Kälte liegt. –
Innsbruck liegt inmitten einer großartigen Gebirgslandschaft. –
Großbritannien liegt auf der Höhe der Nordwestecke des europäischen Kontinents. –
Chicago, das am Michigansee liegt, ist ein wichtiges amerikanisches Atomforschungszentrum.

15 Birmingham, das Großbritanniens zweitgrößte Stadt geworden ist, gehört zu den wichtigsten Industriezentren der Welt. –
Die Unterzeichnung des Staatsvertrages im Jahre 1955 ist eines der bedeutendsten politischen Ereignisse in der Geschichte Österreichs. –
Die internationalen Skirennen, die jährlich in bedeutenden österreichischen Wintersportzentren abgehalten werden, gehören zu den größten Sportveranstaltungen im Lande. –
Das Pferderennen in Epsom, das Fußballcupfinale im Wembley-Stadion, das Rasentennisturnier in Wimbledon, das Bootsrennen auf der Themse und die entscheidenden Kricketspiele sind die hervorragendsten englischen Sportereignisse. –
Die Wiener Messe gehört zu den wichtigsten wirtschaftlichen Veranstaltungen in Österreich. –
Die alljährlich abgehaltenen Festspiele in Edinburgh gehören zu den bemerkenswertesten Musikveranstaltungen in Großbritannien. –
Paris ist eines der hervorragendsten europäischen Kulturzentren. Frankreichs Hauptstadt gilt als eines der bemerkenswertesten Kunst- und Literaturzentren der Welt.

16 Der Stephansdom in Wien und das Goldene Dachl in Innsbruck sind wohl bekannte österreichische Wahrzeichen. –
Die Unabhängigkeitserklärung vom 4. Juli 1776 ist ein Meilenstein in der Geschichte der USA. –
Der Blue Boy, eines der bemerkenswertesten Gemälde in der National Art Gallery in London, gehört zu Thomas Gainsboroughs Meisterwerken. –

---

14 mountain scenery
15 State Treaty; to hold (arrange, organise) a ski-race; trade fair
16 the splitting of an atom; defeat

Die erste Spaltung eines Atoms war nicht nur eine technische Höchstleistung; sie stellte auch einen Meilenstein in der Geschichte der Menschheit dar. –
Die Niederlage der spanischen Armada im Jahre 1588 stellt einen Wendepunkt in der englischen Geschichte dar.

17 Schalter, Drehknöpfe, Druckknöpfe und Tasten sind Vorrichtungen, die zum Unterbrechen und Schließen des elektrischen Stromkreises (Plural!) verwendet werden. –
Turbinen sind Maschinen, die zur Umwandlung von Wasser-, Dampf- oder Gasenergie in Bewegung dienen. –
Ein Thermometer ist ein Instrument, das zum Messen der Temperatur bestimmt ist, während ein Barometer den Luftdruck misst. –
Der Computer wird nicht nur viel in Büros verwendet; die meisten Familien haben einen eigenen PC. Diese Erfindung, die wir uns aus dem modernen Leben nicht mehr wegdenken können, erweist sich als überaus wertvoll. –
Kühlschränke, Staubsauger und Waschmaschinen sind Haushaltsgeräte, deren Verwendung weit verbreitet ist. –
Es ist eine Anlage, die einem doppelten Zweck dient.

18 Es gibt verschiedene Methoden, um Fremdsprachen zu lernen. –
Es gibt zahlreiche Arten von Kräutern und Blüten, die zur Herstellung pharmazeutischer Produkte verwendet werden. –
Es gibt verschiedene Arten von Transportmitteln: Landfahrzeuge, Wasserfahrzeuge, Flugzeuge und Raumschiffe. Das so genannte Hovercraft ist ein Luftkissenfahrzeug. –
Es gibt verschiedene Gruppen von Romanen: historische, biographische, realistische, Abenteuer- und Zukunftsromane.

19 Wir verdanken die Kenntnis vieler Dinge den Massenmedien, wie dem Radio, dem Fernsehen, dem Internet, Filmen, Zeitungen, Zeitschriften und Büchern. –
Unsere wissenschaftlichen Erkenntnisse beruhen auf langwierigen Forschungsarbeiten. –
Die meisten Erfindungen und Entdeckungen sind dem Forschergeist einzelner Menschen zuzuschreiben, wie der berühmte amerikanische Nobelpreisträger John Steinbeck in "A Writer's Credo" feststellte. –

---

17 switch; (to turn) a knob; (to push = to press) a button; a key; to break or to close a circuit ['sɜ:kɪt], air pressure
refrigerator; vacuum cleaner; washing machine; dual

18 herbs and blossoms; pharmaceutical [fɑ:mə'sju:tɪkl]
a (some) means of transport (A.: transportation); a vehicle [vi:ɪkl]; a vessel; an (some) aircraft; a (some) spacecraft; an air cushion [ʊ] vehicle; a futuristic novel, science fiction

19 long research work; the exploring mind; an individual; a Nobel Prize winner

Das berühmte Musical "My Fair Lady" fußt auf George Bernard Shaws Schauspiel "Pygmalion".

20 Dank den modernen Massenmedien ist heutzutage fast jeder mit den wichtigsten Dingen vertraut, die in der Welt vor sich gehen. –
Wenn man einen Führerschein erwerben will, muss man mit der Straßenverkehrsordnung gründlich vertraut sein.

21 William Wordsworths Leben ist untrennbar mit dem Lake District in Nordwestengland verbunden, wo der große Dichter der englischen Romantik geboren wurde, lebte und starb. –
Die Naturwissenschaften stehen untereinander in engem Zusammenhang. –
Heutzutage ist die industrielle Entwicklung mit der Forschung eng verbunden.

22 Bronze ist eine Legierung, die aus Kupfer und Zinn zusammengesetzt ist, während Messing aus Kupfer und Zink besteht. –
"High tea", der in englischen Restaurants und Hotels manchmal am Nachmittag serviert wird, besteht im Wesentlichen aus denselben Gängen wie ein englisches Frühstück. –
Ein Auto besteht im Wesentlichen aus drei Teilen: dem Fahrgestell, der Karosserie und dem Motor.

23 Der Fremdenverkehr spielt im Wirtschaftsleben vieler Länder eine wesentliche Rolle. –
Der Motor spielt im modernen Leben eine wichtige Rolle. –
Trotz vieler Neuerungen spielen gewisse althergebrachte Methoden im täglichen Leben weiterhin eine hervorragende Rolle. –
Zu seiner Zeit spielte Lord Byron eine führende Rolle auf dem Gebiet der Dichtkunst. Er spielte auch im griechischen Freiheitskampf eine aktive Rolle.

24 Der Wintersport, besonders das Skifahren, wird von Jahr zu Jahr beliebter. –
Flugreisen gewinnen von Jahr zu Jahr an Beliebtheit. –
Neue Tendenzen in der Kunst gewinnen immer mehr an Boden.

25 Die Bedeutung des Lernens von Fremdsprachen wird heutzutage voll erkannt. –
Die Notwendigkeit des Energiesparens ist in letzter Zeit in immer mehr Ländern voll erkannt worden.

---

20 to get a driving licence; the Highway Code
22 bronze; alloy; brass; chassis [ˈʃæsɪ]; body
23 tourism, tourist trade, tourist traffic; innovation; traditional struggle for independence

26 Wenn man einen Künstler richtig beurteilen will, muss man etwas über die Zeit und die Verhältnisse wissen, in denen er lebte. –
Um ein Volk gut zu verstehen, müssen wir uns mit seiner Sprache wie mit seinen Sitten und Bräuchen vertraut machen.

27 Aus Zeitungsberichten ist zu entnehmen, dass immer mehr Leute ihren Urlaub im Ausland verbringen.

28 Es war einer der seltsamsten Vorfälle, von denen ich je gehört habe. –
Der Fußballweltcup war eines der spannendsten Sportereignisse, die ich je im Fernsehen verfolgte. –
„Die Zeitmaschine" von Herbert George Wells ist einer der fesselndsten Zukunftsromane, die ich je gelesen habe. –
Die Besteigung des Mount Everest im Himalaya durch Edmund P. Hillary im Jahre 1953 war eines der kühnsten bergsteigerischen Unternehmen in der Geschichte der Menschheit.

29 Zunächst möchte ich das Leben des Dichters behandeln. –
Ich möchte in diesem Zusammenhang erklären, wie diese Anlage arbeitet. –
Wir wollen uns zunächst an die Tage erinnern, an denen jenes historische Ereignis stattfand. –
Zunächst möchte ich Ihre Aufmerksamkeit auf die Tatsache lenken, dass Indien zu jener Zeit noch eine britische Kolonie war.

30 Zunächst, was versteht man unter Automation?

31 Bevor man auf die politische Lage auf diesem Kontinent eingehen kann, müssen mehrere Falktoren berücksichtigt werden, die zu dieser Entwicklung geführt haben. –
Bevor wir auf Einzelheiten eingehen, sollten wir uns über die grundlegenden Fragen dieses Problems im Klaren sein. –
Bevor wir die musikalischen Tendenzen unserer Zeit besprechen, ist es wichtig, dass wir erkennen, was zu dieser Entwicklung geführt hat.

32 In diesem Vortrag möchte ich einen kurzen Überblick über Schottland geben. Ich werde mich in erster Linie mit den Bewohnern und ihren Sitten und Bräuchen beschäftigen; aber ich werde auch eine kurze Beschreibung der Landschaft und der wichtigsten Sehenswürdigkeiten geben. –
In diesem Aufsatz möchte ich eine kurze Inhaltsangabe von Oscar Wildes Lustspiel "An Ideal Husband" geben. Ich will auch einen kurzen Überblick über die verschiedenen Charaktere dieses bekannten Stückes geben.

---

26 circumstance; habits and customs
27 abroad
28 incident; watch, witness; "The Time Machine"; mountaineering expedition
29 system, (industrial) plant

33 Das Thema von John Miltons "Paradise Lost" ist die Erschaffung und der Fall des Menschen sowie die Vertreibung Adams und Evas aus dem Paradies.

34 Der Hauptzweck des Studiums moderner Sprachen ist ihre praktische Beherrschung. Aber das ist nicht das einzige Ziel. Der Student soll auch in das kulturelle und wirtschaftliche Leben der Völker eindringen, deren Sprachen er lernt.

35 "Beowulf", die einzige vorchristliche Sage der Angelsachsen, die erhalten geblieben ist, handelt von den Abenteuern und kühnen Taten eines großen Helden namens Beowulf. –
Dieser Band umfasst ungefähr die Zeit von 1832 bis 1863, die auch frühviktorianische Periode genannt wird. –
Der Artikel behandelt gründlich ein umfangreiches Thema. –
Der Inhalt der Komödie ist:... –
Die Zeitschrift enthält viele farbenprächtige Illustrationen dieses großen Ereignisses.

36 Ein altes englisches Sprichwort sagt, dass Gesundheit besser als Reichtum sei. –
Es besteht ein alter Glaube, dass ein Ungeheuer im Loch Ness hause.

37 Viele Jahrhunderte lang nahm man es als erwiesen an, dass das Atom das kleinste Teilchen sei und nicht gespalten werden könne. –
Viele Jahrhunderte nahm man an, dass die Malaria durch schlechte Luft hervorgerufen werde, bis man schließlich herausfand, dass diese gefährliche Krankheit durch Stechmücken übertragen wird.

---

33 creation and fall; expulsion; Eve [i:v]
34 to penetrate into
35 a pre-Christian saga; to survive; deeds; named; the Early Victorian Period; colourful
36 to dwell
37 particle; to split; mosquito; to transmit

38 Wie unten gezeigt werden wird, ist das Land äußerst reich an Mineralvorkommen. –
Wie vorhin erwähnt wurde, spielen Öl und Schmierfett eine wichtigere Rolle im Leben eines Autos als irgendetwas anderes. –
Das wird jedoch später im Detail behandelt werden. –
Wie oben angegeben, hat Birmingham mehr Einwohner als Glasgow.

39 Hier möchte ich jedoch nicht auf die finanzielle Seite dieses Projektes eingehen.

40 Übrigens vergaß ich zu erwähnen, dass am Ende des Zweiten Weltkrieges Österreich in vier Zonen eingeteilt war: Tirol und Vorarlberg waren von den Franzosen besetzt, Salzburg und der größte Teil Oberösterreichs von den Amerikanern, Kärnten und die Steiermark von den Engländern, Niederösterreich, das Burgenland und ein Teil Oberösterreichs von den Russen. Außerdem war Wien, die Bundeshauptstadt, von Soldaten aller vier Mächte besetzt.

41 In diesem Zusammenhang möchte ich noch etwas erwähnen.

42 Man kann noch hinzufügen, dass defensives Fahren besser ist, als auf seinem Vorrang zu bestehen. –
Eine weitere Bemerkung kann man über die Zweckmäßigkeit dieses Systems hinzufügen.

43 Es bleibt jedoch noch ein weiteres Problem.

44 Wir wollen uns jetzt einer Frage zuwenden, die wir vorher beiseite ließen. –
Wir wollen jetzt überprüfen, wie dieser Mechanismus arbeitet.

45 Ich möchte nun ein anderes Beispiel anführen. –
Als Beweis für den höheren Lebensstandard, den die meisten Menschen in diesem Lande heute genießen, möchte ich einige Beispiele anführen. –
Hier sind einige Punkte, die die Angelegenheit beleuchten.

46 Aber ich will nicht zu lange bei diesem Thema bleiben. –
Aber ich will dieses Thema jetzt fallen lassen. –
Es würde zu weit führen, wenn ich auf Einzelheiten einginge.

47 Hier sind einige Höhepunkte seiner Laufbahn: …

48 Vor allem möchte ich Sie auf die herrliche Landschaft Nordwestschottlands mit ihren einsamen Bergen und “Lochs”, wie die schotti-

---

38 mineral resources; grease
40 greater part of; to occupy
42 defensive driving; right of way; utility
45 matter

schen Seen genannt werden, verweisen. Als Beispiele möchte ich besonders die Insel Skye und die Gegend um den Ben Nevis, Großbritanniens höchsten Berggipfel, erwähnen.

49 Man kann einige Gründe für die Beliebtheit dieses Landes anführen.

50 Es gibt viele derartige Beispiele.

51 Natürlich gibt es Ausnahmen; aber sie sind so selten, dass man sie nicht in Betracht zu ziehen braucht.

52 Dieses Beispiel ist eine Ausnahme, die die Regel bestätigt.

53 Ich habe mich auf diese wenigen Beispiele beschränkt, weil ich glaube, dass sie das Problem genügend beleuchten.

54 All das betrifft die Austauschstudenten.

55 Wie schon der Name sagt, ist das Salzkammergut, das wegen der Schönheit seiner Landschaft berühmt ist, eine jener Gegenden Österreichs, wo Salz gewonnen wird. –
Wie der Titel von T. S. Eliots Drama "Murder in The Cathedral" sagt, handelt das Stück von der Ermordung Thomas Beckets, des Erzbischofs von Canterbury unter Heinrich II.

---

48 mountain top, peak, summit
49 popularity
53 to illustrate
54 exchange student
55 assassination

Certainty or Doubt

56 Ich bin ganz sicher, dass die jungen Leute von heute keineswegs schlechter sind als die Jugend vergangener Generationen. Ich bin sogar völlig überzeugt, dass die überwältigende Mehrheit der heutigen Jugendlichen ein gesundes Verantwortungsgefühl besitzt.

57 Ich weiß aus meiner eigenen Erfahrung: Daheim ist daheim (wörtlich: Es gibt keinen Platz wie daheim [home]).

58 Es ist bekannt, dass das Klima der britischen Inseln stark durch den Golfstrom beeinflusst wird. Daher erscheint es nur natürlich, dass es gleichmäßig, mild und etwas wärmer als das auf der gegenüberliegenden Seite des Kontinents ist.

59 Offensichtlich lieben die Engländer ihre alten, überlieferten Sitten und Uniformen. –
Aller Wahrscheinlichkeit nach ist das britische Parlamentssystem mit dem Unterhaus und dem Oberhaus eines der besten in der Welt.

60 Es ist sehr wahrscheinlich, dass in Zukunft immer mehr Menschen eine höhere Schulbildung erhalten werden. –
Es scheint ziemlich unwahrscheinlich zu sein, dass eines Tages die Eisenbahn vom Auto und Flugzeug ganz verdrängt wird.

61 Das ist besonders beim Motorsport der Fall.

62 Man kann nicht leugnen, dass das metrische System bei weitem einfacher als das alte britische Maß- und Gewichtssystem ist. Es muss jedoch zugegeben werden, dass der Übergang von einem überlieferten zu einem neuen System nicht allzu leicht ist. –
Es versteht sich von selbst, dass die Fußgänger beim Überqueren von Straßen sehr vorsichtig sein müssen. –
Es ist kaum nötig, darauf hinzuweisen, wie wichtig der Fremdenverkehr für die österreichische Wirtschaft ist. –
Es ist unleugbar, dass das große Anwachsen der Weltbevölkerung ernste Probleme mit sich bringt. Es ist unvermeidlich, dass neue Nahrungsmittel gefunden oder erzeugt werden.

63 Es besteht kein Zweifel darüber, dass das disziplinierte Anstellen an Autobushaltestellen, wie es in England üblich ist, sehr vernünftig ist und auf jeden Ausländer einen ausgezeichneten Eindruck macht.

---

56 young people, youngsters, juveniles, the young, youths; by no means; the overwhelming majority; a sound sense of responsibility
58 equable, Gulf Stream
60 education, schooling; to supersede, to displace
62 system of weights and measures; pedestrian; to bring about serious problems; inevitable; foodstuffs
63 to queue up [kju:]; reasonable

64 Zweifellos war die Erfindung der Schiffsschraube durch den österreichischen Techniker Joseph Ressel im Jahre 1827 eine bedeutende technische Leistung.

65 Es ist zweifelhaft, ob der technische Fortschritt die Menschheit glücklicher gemacht hat. –
Es ist unsicher, wie diese Entwicklung weitergehen wird.

66 Es ist eine Tatsache, dass die Ozeane etwa drei Viertel unseres Planeten bedecken. –
Tatsächlich sind viele Verkehrsunfälle dem falschen Verhalten unverantwortlicher Fahrer zuzuschreiben. Natürlich gibt es auch andere Ursachen für Unfälle. –
Es ist eine Tatsache, dass das Atomkraftwerk in Calder Hall in Cumberland die erste Anlage war, die Atomenergie benützte, um Elektrizität für nichtmilitärische Zwecke zu erzeugen.

67 Ich möchte wissen, wie lange der Mensch neue Rekorde in der Leichtathletik aufstellen können wird. –
Wir wissen noch nicht sicher, was der Ursprung und der Zweck von Stonehenge, dem gigantischen Steinkreis in der Nähe von Salisbury, war.

68 Auf den ersten Blick könnte man meinen, dass das Fernsehen nur Vorteile habe, aber bei genauerer Überlegung wird man sicherlich finden, dass es auch gewisse Nachteile hat. –
Beim ersten Durchlesen eines einfachen englischen Textes scheint es, dass das Erlernen des Englischen sehr leicht sei; aber nach sorgfältigem Studium wird Folgendes klar: Je mehr man in die Sprache eindringt, desto mehr sieht man sich beträchtlichen Schwierigkeiten gegenüber.

69 Auf alle Fälle erleichtert ein gutes Transportsystem die Verteilung der Waren. –
Jedenfalls wird nach (in) englischem Recht eine angeklagte Person so lange als unschuldig betrachtet und behandelt, bis sie einer Schuld überführt ist.

70 Auf keinen Fall sollten wir vergessen, dass wir im Ausland Vertreter unseres Vaterlandes sind.

---

64 the ship's propeller; engineer; a technical achievement, an engineering feat
65 humanity
66 conduct; irresponsible; plant; nuclear power station; civilian
67 athletics; man; to establish a record, to set up a record; gigantic; stone circle, Salisbury, ['sɒ:lzbərɪ]
68 to penetrate into; to be faced with
69 distribution; accused; to be considered and treated as innocent; to prove guilty
70 representative; native country: when abroad

OPINION OR FEELING

71 Während nach unserer Meinung einige englische Speisen wenig schmackhaft sind, sind gewisse kontinentale Speisen für den Geschmack der Engländer zu sehr gewürzt. Ich für meine Person bevorzuge das englische Frühstück und das kontinentale Mittag- und Abendessen.

72 Ich habe manchmal den Eindruck, dass viele Menschen ihre Gesundheit für so selbstverständlich halten, dass sie sich kaum Gedanken um eine richtige Lebensweise machen. –
Ich bin der Meinung, dass CD-ROMs das Erlernen fremder Sprachen nicht nur erleichtern, sondern auch angenehmer machen.

73 Vermutlich wird uns mein Londoner Freund, bei dessen Familie ich während der Sommerferien wohnte, nächstes Jahr in Österreich besuchen.

74 Nach seinem Äußeren zu schließen, kann man annehmen, dass er ein wohlhabender Herr ist. –
Aus der gegenwärtigen Weltwirtschaftslage kann man schließen, dass die Konjunktur weiter anhalten wird.

75 Vor der entscheidenden Schlacht bei Trafalgar gegen Napoleons Flotte im Jahre 1805 soll der berühmte britische Admiral Lord Horatio Nelson ausgerufen haben: „England erwartet, dass jeder Mann seine Pflicht tut." –
Er soll in Kanada sein.

76 Ich muss zugeben, dass es nicht leicht ist, sich in einem fremden Land zurechtzufinden, ohne eine Ahnung von der Sprache zu haben, die dort gesprochen wird. –
Ich bin nicht bereit zuzugeben, dass Österreichs Fußball weit unter dem internationalen Niveau ist, wenngleich eingestanden werden muss, dass es mehrere Nationen gibt, die mehr Klassespieler haben als unser kleines Land.

77 Ich kann nicht umhin zu erwähnen, dass die Amerikaner gastfreundlicher und geselliger als die meisten Europäer sind.

78 Ob Sie es glauben oder nicht, er legte diese Strecke in weniger als einer halben Stunde zurück. –

---

71 a little insipid; seasoned, spicy
72 to take so much for granted; to give little thought to; a proper way of living
74 appearance; well-to-do; (economic) boom
76 to find one's way about; standards; first-rate player
77 hospitable; sociable
78 to cover a distance

So seltsam es scheinen mag, bin ich doch davon überzeugt, dass es wahr ist.

79 Ich finde es schwer, mir vorzustellen, dass so etwas geschehen ist. Offen gesagt, glaube ich es überhaupt nicht. –
Ich zögere nicht zu glauben, dass jemand dort gelandet ist.

80 Kondition ist alles. Das gilt für jede Art von Sport.

81 Was für das Französische gilt, muss notwendigerweise bis zu einem gewissen Grad auch für die anderen romanischen Sprachen gelten.

82 In Wirklichkeit trifft genau das Gegenteil zu.

83 Obwohl es ziemlich unglaubwürdig klingt, ist es doch wahr.

84 Kürzere Arbeitszeiten und bessere Arbeitsbedingungen sind dem raschen technischen Fortschritt zuzuschreiben, ohne den die beträchtlichen sozialen Verbesserungen ganz unmöglich wären. –
Der Rhythmus eines Verses ist der regelmäßigen Wiederkehr der Betonung oder des Akzentes zuzuschreiben.

85 Die Tatsache, dass nur weibliche Glühwürmchen glühen, erklärt das weibliche Geschlecht des Wortes „Glühwürmchen" im Englischen. –
Die Möglichkeit, in Städten höhere Löhne bei kürzeren Arbeitszeiten zu verdienen, erklärt zum Teil das Problem der Landflucht.

86 Bei vielen Industrieprodukten ist es ausschließlich eine Frage des persönlichen Geschmackes, welchem Fabrikat man den Vorzug gibt. –
Inwieweit man allen Moderichtungen zu folgen wünscht, ist eine Angelegenheit der persönlichen Einstellung.

87 Hier erhebt sich die Frage, ob die Zeit für ein weltweites Abrüsten schon gekommen ist. –
Es bestehen Meinungsverschiedenheiten, ob Shakespeare wirklich der Autor aller Stücke war, die ihm zugeschrieben werden.

88 Katastrophen, verursacht durch Überschwemmungen, Erdbeben oder Orkane, beweisen, dass es auch in unserem technischen Zeitalter Dinge gibt, die jenseits der menschlichen Kontrolle liegen.

89 Ich kann sein Verhalten nicht verstehen; es ist unvereinbar mit seinem Charakter.

90 Vieles spricht für die Düsenflugzeuge. –

---

81 the Romance languages
84 recurrence; stress
85 glow-worm; gender; wages; rural depopulation, rural exodus
86 make; modern trend; attitude, approach
87 disarmament
88 catastrophe [kə'tæstrəfɪ]; flood [ʌ]; earthqake; hurricane
89 conduct, behaviour
90 jet plane; the abusive taking of; tablet; pill

Vieles spricht gegen die missbräuchliche Einnahme von Tabletten und Pillen.

91 Es ist von äußerster Wichtigkeit, dass jeder Verkehrsteilnehmer immer diszipliniert ist und sich richtig verhält. –
Es ist überaus wichtig, dass wir auch den Standpunkt anderer einsehen (= sehen) und berücksichtigen.

92 Es ist nicht wesentlich, ob wir diese Methode oder eine ähnliche anwenden.

93 Heutzutage ist es für viele Menschen unerlässlich, wenigstens eine Fremdsprache zu können.

94 Man sollte diesen Bemerkungen nicht zu viel Bedeutung beimessen. –
Auch nach dem Verlassen der Schule sollte man weder seine geistige noch seine körperliche Ausbildung vernachlässigen. –
Es wäre ein böser Fehler, seine eigene Leistungsfähigkeit zu überschätzen. Natürlich sollte man sie auch nicht zu sehr unterschätzen.

95 Beim Lernen moderner Sprachen sollte auf das Sprechen ein gebührender Nachdruck gelegt werden. Besonders sollte auf eine richtige Aussprache und Intonation geachtet werden.

96 Nach den Gesetzen der Wirtschaft müssen eine geringe Anlieferung und eine große Nachfrage nach Waren unweigerlich zu Preissteigerungen führen. Andererseits werden ein großes Angebot und eine geringe Nachfrage Preissenkungen verursachen. –
Wie wir in den letzten Jahren häufig gesehen haben, müssen neue Maschinen nicht Arbeitslosigkeit zur Folge haben. Im Gegenteil, manche von ihnen schaffen neue Arbeitsplätze.

97 Es mag sein, dass diese Maßnahmen nicht populär sind; aber sie sind für die wirtschaftliche Gesundung des Landes unerlässlich. –
Es ist wahr, dass viele Leute die zeitgenössische Kunst nicht würdigen können. Es mag sein, dass die Kunst wirklich dem Zeitalter voraus ist, in dem sie geschaffen wird. Aber manchmal scheint es, dass auch moderne Produkte, die nur wenig mit Kunst zu tun haben, ausgestellt oder aufgeführt werden.

98 Es wäre zwecklos uns vorzustellen, wie die Welt heute aussehen würde, wenn bestimmte historische Ereignisse nicht stattgefunden hätten.

99 Glücklicherweise ist das selten der Fall. –
Gott sei Dank wurde niemand bei diesem Unfall verletzt.

---

94 mental; physical training; capabilities, efficiency
96 supply; demand for merchandise (= goods); offer; increase (reduction) in prices
97 measure; economic recovery; contemporary art; to be ahead of; to exhibit; to perform
98 *what* is it like?
99 to 'injure

100 Glücklicherweise erfreuen sich viele Menschen unserer Zeit eines relativ hohen Lebensstandards. Leider gibt es andererseits noch riesige unterentwickelte Gebiete in der Welt.

101 Es ist überaus bedauerlich, dass es Leute gibt, die die Natur verunstalten, indem sie Abfälle achtlos wegwerfen. Wie schade, dass nicht jeder dazu beiträgt, die natürliche Schönheit der Landschaft zu bewahren.

---

100 an underdeveloped area
101 to spoil; waste; to preserve

General Statement and Classification

102 Allgemein gesehen, beeinflusst die Londoner Börse das Wohlergehen jedes britischen Bürgers, da sie eine Funktion ausübt, die für das Wirtschaftsleben des Landes – für das Geschäftsleben, die Industrie und die Regierung – absolut wesentlich ist. –
Historisch gesehen, bezeichnet der Tod Königin Viktorias im Jahre 1901 das Ende einer Periode, die reich an politischen, sozialen, industriellen und wissenschaftlichen Veränderungen war. –
Im weitesten Sinne sind viele Amerikaner Europäer; denn sie sind entweder selbst Europäer oder Nachkommen von Europäern. –
Vergleichsweise ist das Leben in Frankreich sehr teuer.

103 „Das Eis brechen“ bedeutet im ursprünglichen und wörtlichen Sinn „die gefrorene Oberfläche eines Flusses, Sees oder Meeres für die Durchfahrt von Schiffen brechen“. In übertragener Bedeutung jedoch bezeichnet diese Wendung dasselbe wie „der formellen und steifen Atmosphäre bei einem gesellschaftlichen Treffen ein Ende bereiten“.

104 Das würde ich ein interessantes Experiment nennen. –
Dieser Autor ist, was ich einen repräsentativen Dichter unseres Jahrhunderts nennen würde.

105 Der Mond ist sozusagen eine permanente Raumstation.

106 Kurz, jene, die sich leicht anpassen können, werden im Leben Erfolg haben. –
Mit einem Wort, es ist nicht leicht, ein guter Verlierer zu sein.

107 Eine Sprache wird am besten durch praktische Übung gelernt, mit anderen Worten, die vier Sprachfertigkeiten des Zuhörens, Sprechens, Lesens und Schreibens müssen immer wieder geübt werden, bis man eine brauchbare Kenntnis der Sprache erworben hat. –
Um es anders und vielleicht genauer auszudrücken, es ist die Aufgabe des Vergasers, den Treibstoff zu zerstäuben und ihn mit der richtigen Luftmenge zu mischen.

108 Unter keinen Bedingungen würde ich eine solche Stelle annehmen.

109 Unter äußerst günstigen Bedingungen kann ein Hubschrauber dort landen.

---

102 welfare; citizen, subject; to perform a function; descendant
103 surface; passage; idiom; formal; stiff; to put an end to; a social meeting
105 space station
106 to adapt oneself to
107 practice; language skill; to acquire a working knowledge; carburettor; fuel; to atomise; the right amount
108 position, situation, post, job
109 helicopter

110 Für morgen wird eine Sonnenfinsternis erwartet. Für diesen besonderen Umstand ist es ratsam, Sonnenbrillen und ein Fernglas oder ein Fernrohr bereitzuhalten.

111 Bei dieser Gelegenheit werde ich der Insel Man einen Besuch abstatten.

112 In diesem Falle würde ich mich weigern hinzufahren.

113 In mancher Hinsicht ist eine Reise nach Schottland lohnender als nach Wales.

114 Im Notfall werden wir dort die Reise unterbrechen müssen.

115 Der Südwesten Englands zieht in steigendem Maße große Urlaubermengen nicht nur aus dem Londoner Gebiet, sondern aus ganz Großbritannien an. –
Die Wirtschaft der meisten europäischen Länder hängt in viel größerem Maße von ihren Industriegütern als von ihren landwirtschaftlichen Erzeugnissen ab.

116 Wie es häufig der Fall ist, wurden seine Leistungen in seiner Heimat weniger geschätzt als im Ausland.

117 Das heißt nicht, dass ich gegen Autotouren bin; es heißt nur, dass ich es hasse, einfach von einem Gasthaus zum anderen zu fahren.

118 Es ließe sich auch etwas über gewisse Nachteile dieser Methode sagen.

119 Es ist bemerkenswert, dass die Vereinigten Staaten größere Bodenschätze als irgend ein anderes Gebiet gleicher Größe haben. Es ist auch erwähnenswert, dass das Land genauso mannigfaltig wie ausgedehnt ist: Es gibt Ebenen und Gebirge, Wiesen und Wälder, Sandboden und Tonerde und fette, dunkle Lehmböden. Während in einer Gegend des Landes den Großteil des Jahres über Sonnenschein herrscht, ist eine andere durch kaltes, regnerisches Wetter im Sommer und tiefe Schneemassen im Winter gekennzeichnet. –
Am meisten interessiere ich mich für die Sitten und Bräuche fremder Völker.

120 Es ist überraschend, dass der australische Kontinent noch immer von relativ wenigen Menschen bewohnt wird. –
Es ist fast unglaublich, welche Kraft dem Menschen durch die Hoffnung gegeben wird. –

---

110 eclipse of the sun; advisable; sun-glasses; binoculars; telescope; to provide
112 to refuse
113 rewarding
114 to break a journey
115 crowds of holiday-makers; manufactured goods; agricultural produce
119 mineral resources; varied; vast; sandy soil; clay; rich loam; snows; habits and customs
120 to inhabit

121 Die so genannten “enclosures” sind für die Landschaft Großbritanniens charakteristisch. Durch sie wird das Land in einzelne Grundstücke unterteilt: im Süden meist mittels Busch- und Strauchhecken, im Norden mittels Steinreihen. –
Es ist für den englischen Tee typisch, dass er so stark ist, dass man ihn nicht ohne Milch trinkt.

122 Shakespeares Werke zeichnen sich durch ihren freimütigen Realismus aus.

123 Sein Aufenthalt in den Vereinigten Staaten hat seine Aussprache beeinflusst. Er spricht jetzt Englisch mit einem amerikanischen Akzent. –
Die großen technischen Fortschritte, die in jüngster Zeit gemacht worden sind, haben das menschliche Leben in beträchtlichem Maße beeinflusst. –
Die Erfindung des Radars hatte einen großen Einfluss auf die Schifffahrt und das Flugwesen. –
Leider wurde der Besuch der Freilichtaufführung durch das trübe Wetter stark beeinträchtigt.

124 Moderne Transportmittel erleichtern das Reisen beträchtlich. Sie befähigen uns, an jeden beliebigen Ort des Erdballs zu gelangen. –
Die Verwendung des UKW-Bereiches im Rundfunk hat die Qualität des Radioempfanges sehr verbessert. –
Es ist Tatsache, dass der Rauch von Fabriken sowie die Auspuffgase von Motorfahrzeugen die Luft in den Industriestädten in gefährlichem Maße verschlechtern. –
Das moderne Leben macht die Spezialisierung der meisten Menschen auf ein bestimmtes Gebiet notwendig. –
Das vereinfacht die Angelegenheit. –
Richtige Pflege gewährleistet eine lange Lebensdauer Ihres Autos.

125 Jeder Mensch und jedes Land sollten es sich zur Aufgabe machen, die Völkerverständigung zu fördern. –
Sorglose Planung erhöht die Produktionskosten; gute Planung vermindert sie. –
Elektronische Rechenmaschinen beschleunigen die Büroarbeit beträchtlich; sie erlauben es, dass hunderte Rechnungen in einer Sekunde durchgeführt werden können. –

---

121 plot of land, estate; shrub; hedge
122 frank
123 navigation; aviation; attendance; open air performance
124 a (some) means of transport (A.: transportation); globe; the v.h.f. range (very high frequency); broadcasting; radio reception; exhaust gas; motor vehicle; specialisation in; care; long life
125 production costs; electronic computer; calculation, to do sums; growth

Das milde Klima, das an der Südküste Cornwalls herrscht, begünstigt den Wuchs tropischer Pflanzen, wie Palmen, Bananen und Zitronen. – Ein eleganter Swimmingpool vergrößert den Komfort des Ozeanriesen.

126 Sicherheitsvorrichtungen in Fabriken verhindern Unfälle. Natürlich ist auch das richtige Verhalten des Maschinenarbeiters zur Ausschaltung von Gefahren und zur Vermeidung von Unfällen wesentlich.

127 In unseren Tagen geschieht viel, um die Sicherheit auf den Straßen zu gewährleisten und um die Gefahr von Verkehrsunfällen herabzusetzen.

128 Dieses dringende Bedürfnis hat zur Eröffnung von Informationszentren geführt. –
Die rasche Industrialisierung im 19. Jahrhundert, die zum Entstehen vieler Städte führte, brachte große soziale Probleme mit sich.

129 Intensive Forschungsarbeiten (Singular!) haben wesentlich zu den beträchtlichen Fortschritten beigetragen, die in den letzten Jahrzehnten erzielt worden sind. –
Die hervorragenden Übersetzungen durch A. W. Schlegel und L. Tieck haben sehr zur vollen Wertschätzung Shakespeares in den deutschsprachigen Ländern beigetragen.

130 Viele Sprachwissenschaftler glauben, dass sich Sprachlabors für die rasche Aneignung guter praktischer Kenntnisse moderner Sprachen als überaus wertvoll erweisen.

131 Nach meiner Meinung kommt nichts einem Sonnenaufgang in den Alpen gleich. –
Als Dramatiker ist William Shakespeare zweifellos unübertroffen. –
Als Sir Walter Scott herausfand, dass seine Verse gegenüber Lord Byrons Dichtung ungünstig abschnitten, wandte er sich dem Roman zu.

132 Moderne Maschinen helfen, den steigenden Bedarf zu decken. –
Die Ausstellung entsprach allen Erwartungen der zahlreichen Besucher. –
Hoffen wir, dass die Nahrungsmittelerzeugung den stets steigenden Bedarf der rasch wachsenden Weltbevölkerung decken kann.

133 Kunststoff wird auf diesem und auf verwandten Gebieten viel verwendet. –
Die Wasserkraft wird in vielen Teilen Österreichs erfolgreich ausgenützt.

---

126 safety device; conduct; machine operator, machinist
128 opening
129 intense; appreciation
130 linguist; language laboratory; the acquisition of a good working knowledge

134 Das LD-Verfahren, die in Linz und Donawitz entwickelte Methode der Stahlerzeugung, ist in vielen Ländern der Welt eingeführt worden. Überall, wo diese Technik oder eine ihrer Modifikationen verwendet wird, erweist sie sich den bisherigen Verfahren überlegen. –
Die Bacontheorie, derzufolge der englische Philosoph Francis Bacon Shakespeares Werke geschrieben haben soll, wird allgemein verworfen.

135 Es gibt mehrere wesentliche Unterschiede zwischen der romantischen Bewegung in England und jener in Frankreich. Der auffallendste ist, dass hier (im letztgenannten Land) das Ereignis bewusst erlebt wurde, während es dort (im erstgenannten) instinktiv erfasst wurde. –
Es bestehen einige grundlegende Ähnlichkeiten zwischen diesen beiden Methoden.

136 20 Guineas entsprechen 21 Pfund. –
110 Yards entsprechen ungefähr 100 Metern. –
Das entspricht der Gesamtbevölkerung Europas.

137 Das Ohm'sche Gesetz stellt fest, dass die Stromstärke gleich der elektrischen Spannung dividiert durch den elektrischen Widerstand ist. Mit anderen Worten, die Stromstärke ist direkt proportional der Spannung und verkehrt proportional dem Widerstand. –
Seine Einstellung steht in scharfem Gegensatz zur Meinung vieler seiner Zeitgenossen. –
Im Norden und Westen Großbritanniens ist der Boden ganz anders als im Süden und Osten.

138 Wir können zwischen Tageszeitungen, Wochenzeitungen, vierzehntägig erscheinenden Zeitungen, Monatszeitschriften und vierteljährlich erscheinenden Schriften unterscheiden. –
Wir wollen die Vorzüge und die Nachteile des Stadtlebens und des Landlebens einander gegenüberstellen.

139 Die menschliche Geschichte kann man wie folgt einteilen: Altertum, Mittelalter, Neuzeit und jüngste Geschichte. –
Zeitschriften kann man auf verschiedene Arten einteilen. –
Metalle können in folgende zwei Gruppen eingeteilt werden: Eisenmetalle und Nichteisenmetalle.

140 Zum alpinen Skilauf gehören der Abfahrtslauf, der Torlauf und der Riesentorlauf. –

---

134 traditional
135 conscious
137 Ohm's law; current; voltage, tension, e.m.f. (electro-motive force); resistance; attitude, approach; contemporary; soil
138 daily; weekly; fortnightly; monthly; quarterly
139 Antiquity; the Middle Ages; modern times; recent history; non-ferrous metals
140 Alpine skiing; downhill = downhill run; (giant) slalom; full back; half back; forward

Zu einer Fußballmannschaft gehören folgende Spieler: der Tormann, die Verteidiger, die Mittelfeldspieler und die Stürmer.

141 Wie alles andere hat das Fernsehen sowohl Vorteile als auch Nachteile. –
Wir wollen zunächst die Vorteile betrachten. –
Hier sind einige der Hauptvorteile, die die Arbeitsteilung bietet. Ich will auch einige Nachteile erwähnen, die dieses System hat.

142 Verschiedene Schwierigkeiten treten beim Simultandolmetschen auf. –
Verschiedene Probleme müssen noch angepackt und gelöst werden.

143 Zuerst müssen wir unsere Vorurteile loswerden.

144 Alle diese Hilfsmittel stehen uns heute zur Verfügung.

145 Der Glaube an das Leben und an die menschliche Natur spiegelt sich in allen Werken Charles Dickens' wider.

146 Vieles in Edgar Allan Poes Werk beweist seine Vorliebe für das Mystische, das Übernatürliche und das Schreckliche.

147 Wie groß seine Kunst war, kann man am besten ersehen, wenn man seine Werke mit denen seiner Zeitgenossen vergleicht.

148 Newtons Größe als Naturwissenschaftler beruht auf seiner berühmten Gravitationstheorie.

---

141 division of labour
142 simultaneous interpretation
143 prejudice
147 contemporary
148 theory of gravitation

149 Am Beginn des 18. Jahrhunderts, genau gesagt im Jahre 1707, wurden England und Schottland vereinigt.
150 Als das 17. Jahrhundert zu Ende ging, wurde in England die Pressefreiheit gesetzlich verankert.
151 Viele große Erfindungen in der Stahlindustrie gehen bis in die erste Hälfte des 18. Jahrhunderts zurück.
152 Die Entdeckungen des auslaufenden 15. und beginnenden 16. Jahrhunderts leiteten eine neue Epoche in der Geschichte der Menschheit ein.
153 In der unmittelbaren Nachkriegsperiode sahen sich fast alle europäischen Länder beträchtlichen Wiederaufbauproblemen gegenüber.
154 Gegenwärtig besitzen wir viele Dinge, von denen unsere Vorfahren nicht einmal geträumt haben. –
Heutzutage ist der Umweltschutz ein lebenswichtiges Problem. Daher werden in vielen Ländern Maßnahmen gegen die Umweltverschmutzung, wie die Wasserverschmutzung oder die Luftverschmutzung, getroffen.
155 Früher war es (matters were = things were) ganz anders. –
Während der Regierung Maria Theresias wurden viele entscheidende Reformen durchgeführt.
156 Neulich traf ich am Abend meinen schottischen Freund. Ich werde ihn heute in 14 Tagen wiedersehen.
157 Gleichzeitig fand ein Tennisturnier statt.
158 Inzwischen waren einige Polizisten eingetroffen.
159 Von Zeit zu Zeit hörte man ein seltsames Geräusch.
160 Derzeit sehe ich keine Möglichkeit, wie das erreicht werden könnte.
161 Im Laufe der Zeit konnte er sich ein reiches Wissen auf diesem Gebiet aneignen.
162 Zuerst benützte (= nahm) ich den Zug nach Salzburg. Dann fuhr ich mit dem Autobus zum Flugplatz. Schließlich benützte ich das Flugzeug nach London.
163 Bisher sind die Wetterberichte nicht absolut verlässlich gewesen.
164 Damals fanden die Olympischen Spiele in Innsbruck statt.
165 Vor dieser Zeit dachte man, die Erde sei eine flache Scheibe.

---

150 freedom of the Press; legal; to establish
152 to inaugurate
153 to be faced with; reconstruction
154 ancestors; protection of the environment; environmental (water, air) pollution; vital
157 tournament
163 weather forecast; reliable
165 flat; disk, disc

CONCLUSION

166 Zusammenfassend kann man sagen, dass man nur hoffen kann, dass die Atomkraft ausschließlich für friedliche Zwecke verwendet werden wird. –
Abschließend möchte ich noch einmal betonen: Heutzutage ist eine bessere Völkerverständigung notwendiger denn je zuvor in der Geschichte der Menschheit.

167 Im Großen und Ganzen glaube ich, dass es richtig ist zu behaupten, dass der Lebensstandard vieler Europäer in unseren Tagen weitaus höher ist als je in der Vergangenheit.

168 Wenn man seine Vorzüge und Nachteile abwägt, kann man zu dem Schluss kommen, dass das Fernsehen, solange es vernünftig verwendet wird, eine nützliche Erfindung ist, die Information, Bildung und Unterhaltung bietet.

169 So haben wir gesehen, welch wichtige Rolle die Hoffnung im menschlichen Leben spielt.

170 Aus den angegebenen Gründen bin ich für ein Vereintes Europa.

171 In diesem Aufsatz habe ich mich bemüht zu beweisen, dass die Zufriedenheit das Wichtigste im menschlichen Leben ist.

172 Was immer die Zukunft bringen mag, eines ist sicher: Was aus uns werden wird, hängt in großem Maße von uns selbst ab. –
Wenn wir weiter in die Zukunft blicken, besteht Grund zur Annahme, dass es schließlich der Medizin gelingen wird, noch mehr menschliche Krankheiten zu heilen und viele andere zu lindern.

173 Nur so wird es möglich sein, dieses Ziel zu erreichen.

174 Zollen wir daher jenen Anerkennung, die sich bemüht haben, dieses Problem zu lösen.

175 Das mag eine Möglichkeit für die ferne Zukunft sein.

---

166 nuclear power, atomic energy; exclusively; peaceful; a better mutual understanding among nations
168 entertainment
171 satisfaction
172 to cure; to soothe, to relieve
173 to attain an end (= a goal)
174 to endeavour

PREPOSITIONS AND GROUP PREPOSITIONS*

P 1 Abgesehen von seiner Pflicht, die Königin über die Regierungsgeschäfte zu informieren, führt der englische Ministerpräsident den Vorsitz über das Kabinett und spricht im Unterhaus über die wichtigsten Regierungsangelegenheiten.

P 2 Viele Engländer verbringen ihren Sommerurlaub in einem der zahlreichen Küstenorte ihres Landes. Bei den Londonern sind die Seebäder am Ärmelkanal besonders beliebt.

P 3 Angesichts des großen Erfolges wurde das Musical "My Fair Lady" im ältesten Theater Londons, Drury Lane, mehr als sechs Jahre lang aufgeführt.

P 4 Anstatt alkoholischer Getränke oder alkoholfreier Säfte ist der Tee das bevorzugte Getränk der Engländer.

P 5 Beim LD-Verfahren wird reiner Sauerstoff vertikal auf das Metallbad geblasen. –
Auf allen englischen Münzen und Briefmarken befindet sich das Porträt eines englischen Herrschers.

P 6 Auf Grund seines leichten Gewichtes wird das Aluminium im Flugzeugbau viel verwendet.

P 7 Die britischen Inseln liegen auf der Höhe der Nordwestecke des europäischen Kontinents.

P 8 Er schrieb uns aus Neuseeland.

P 9 Er rief aus der Höhle heraus.

P 10 Alle Gesetzesanträge außer Finanzgesetzesanträgen müssen vom Oberhaus genehmigt werden. –
Mit Ausnahme Eduards V. und Eduards VIII. sind alle englischen Könige und Königinnen seit 1066 in der Westminster Abtei gekrönt worden. –
Außer Konzerten finden in der Royal Albert Hall auch andere

---

* The references are to the prepositions and group prepositions, e.g.: gegen P 25.
P 1 duty; the business of the Government; to preside over
P 2 seaside place, seaside resort
P 4 alcoholic beverage; soft drink (non-alcoholic)
P 5 pure oxygen; metal bath; sovereign
P 6 aircraft construction
P 9 cave
P 10 (money) bill; to pass; ball; boxing exhibition

öffentliche Veranstaltungen, wie Bälle und Boxveranstaltungen, statt.

P 11 Eine große Menschenmenge wartete außerhalb der Kirche auf die Neuvermählten.

P 12 Seit einigen Jahren arbeitet er bei der Firma Brown. – Bath, der berühmte römische Badeort, liegt bei Bristol. – Bei der Vorbereitung einer Reise sollte man nicht vergessen, dass man mehr Geld, aber weniger Bekleidung als ursprünglich geplant braucht. – Heutzutage helfen uns alle Arten Maschinen bei unserer Arbeit.

P 13 Bereits im Jahre 1939 führte der Engländer J. L. Baird seine Farbfernsehmethode vor.

P 14 Alle diese Entdeckungen wurden binnen weniger Jahrzehnte gemacht.

P 15 Die Vereinigten Staaten erstrecken sich vom Atlantik bis zum Pazifik und von den Großen Seen bis zum Golf von Mexiko. – Im Königlichen Shakespearetheater von Stratford-upon-Avon wird jedes Jahr von April bis Ende November eine Auswahl von Shakespearestücken aufgeführt. – Obwohl die anderen bis Mitternacht dort bleiben, ist sie gewöhnlich bis 11 Uhr zurück.

P 16 Er näherte sich ihnen bis auf wenige Yards.

P 17 Ich fuhr mit dem Zug bis nach Bregenz. Ich blieb dort bis nach Ostern.

P 18 Dank seiner großen Energie hatte er schließlich Erfolg.

P 19 Man findet diese Blumen nur diesseits des Gebirges.

P 20 An belebten Straßenkreuzungen wird der Verkehr durch Verkehrsampeln geregelt. – In Kent's Cavern in Devon führen erfahrene Führer die Besucher durch ein Labyrinth von Gängen und Grotten, die einst von prähistorischen Tieren und primitiven Menschen bewohnt wurden.

P 21 Mein amerikanischer Freund reiste durch ganz Europa.

P 22 Bitte geben Sie die Preise einschließlich aller Abgaben an.

P 11 the newly-weds
P 12 Messrs Brown ['mesəz]; spa; remember; originally planned
P 13 to demonstrate
P 15 to extend; Gulf; selection; to perform
P 18 to succeed
P 20 a busy crossing, crossroads; traffic lights ; traffic signals; automatic signals; to control; experienced; guide; passage; a grotto, some grottoes; in ancient times; to occupy
P 22 quote; charges

P 23 Erst im Jahre 1867 wurde Alaska von Russland an die USA verkauft. –
Die Römer, die das erste Mal im Jahr 55 v. Chr. unter Julius Caesar nach Britannien gekommen waren, verließen das Land erst 410 n. Chr. für immer.

P 24 Während die Regierungspartei für das Projekt war, stimmte die Opposition dagegen. –
Viele Wissenschaftler haben für den menschlichen Fortschritt große Opfer gebracht. –
Ich bekam diese Bilder für die Fotos, die ich ihm geschickt hatte.

P 25 Das ist gegen die Regeln. –
Das Fußballspiel Österreich gegen Schottland wird in Glasgow stattfinden. Die österreichische Mannschaft wird gegen die ausgezeichneten Schotten schwer zu kämpfen haben. –
Mehrere Raketen sind zum Mond geschickt worden. –
Gegen Ende des 6. Jahrhunderts wurde in England das Christentum eingeführt.

P 26 An klaren Tagen kann man von Calais, das in einer Entfernung von etwa 20 Meilen Dover gegenüberliegt, die britische Küste sehen. –
Der neue Entwurf hat mehrere Vorzüge gegenüber älteren Plänen.

P 27 Gemäß den Bestimmungen des Jugendherbergsverbandes darf niemand mehr als drei aufeinander folgende Nächte in einer Herberge bleiben.

P 28 Gleich nach meiner Ankunft in London fuhr ich zu meinen englischen Freunden in Surrey.

P 29 Es war für mich ein angenehmes Erlebnis, die Themse hinaufzufahren.
In Österreich gibt es zahlreiche Seilbahnen und Sessellifte, die die Touristen auf prachtvolle Berggipfel bringen.

P 30 Hinsichtlich seiner Regierungsform ist das Vereinigte Königreich von Großbritannien und Nordirland eine konstitutionelle Monarchie. –
Hinsichtlich der landschaftlichen Schönheiten gibt es nur wenige Länder, die sich mit Tirol messen können.

P 23 for good = for ever; 55 B.C.; 410 A.D.
P 24 to make sacrifices
P 25 Christianity
P 26 at a distance of; design
P 27 regulation; Youth Hostels Association; consecutive
P 29 cable-railway, cable-car; chair lift
P 30 form of government; constitutional monarchy; scenic [si:] beauty; to be compared to

P 31 Der Motor ist hinter dem Kühler und unter der Motorhaube.

P 32 Plötzlich fühlten wir, dass uns jemand hinter einem Busch beobachtete.

P 33 Wir gingen zum Hafen hinunter.

P 34 Im Falle eines Brandes benützen Sie die Notausgänge!

P 35 Im Gegensatz zu den meisten Ländern der Welt bewegt sich der Straßenverkehr in Großbritannien auf der linken Seite.

P 36 Er sprach im Namen der britischen Regierung.

P 37 Im Vergleich zum Durchschnittswert gab es in diesem Jahr zu viel Regen.

P 38 Im Verhältnis zu seiner Größe ist Australien wenig (=dünn) besiedelt.

P 39 Immer mehr Probleme treten im Zusammenhang mit der Weltraumforschung auf.

P 40 Es ist nicht leicht, diese Broschüre ins Deutsche zu übersetzen. – In der St. Pauls-Kathedrale, der größten Leistung des berühmtesten englischen Baumeisters Christopher Wren, befinden sich die Grabmäler Wellingtons, des Siegers von Waterloo, und Nelsons, des Helden von Trafalgar. –.
Der Coloradofluss mündet (= fließt) in den Golf von Kalifornien. – Es gibt verschiedene Methoden, um Eisen in Stahl umzuwandeln.

P 41 In Anbetracht ihrer hervorragenden Leistungen auf dem Gebiete der Medizin wurde zwischen den beiden Weltkriegen drei österreichischen Ärzten der Nobelpreis verliehen.

P 42 Die Regeln in Bezug auf die Verwendung der Interpunktionszeichen sind im Englischen weniger streng als im Deutschen.

P 43 In nächster Nähe der Westminster Abtei ist die St. Margaret Kirche, die Pfarrkirche des Unterhauses.

P 44 Infolge starker (= schwerer) Regenfälle gab es in mehreren Teilen des Landes verheerende Überschwemmungen.

P 45 Diese Fabrik verkauft ihre Erzeugnisse in der ganzen Welt.
Der berühmte englische Komponist Benjamin Britten ist in der ganzen Welt bekannt.

P 31 engine; radiator; bonnet (A.: hood)
P 34 fire; emergency exit
P 37 mean value, average value
P 38 to populate
P 39 to arise; space exploration
P 40 brochure; crowning achievement; tomb [tu:m]; victor; to convert
P 42 punctuation mark; rigid
P 43 parish church
P 44 disastrous; flood
P 45 output; composer

P 46 Innsbrucks Lage inmitten einer herrlichen Gebirgslandschaft ist einzigartig. –
Mitten im Leben sind wir vom Tode umfangen. (= Inmitten des Lebens sind wir im Tode.)

P 47 Innerhalb des Zylinders befindet sich der Kolben.

P 48 In Übereinstimmung mit den gegenwärtigen Verordnungen muss jeder Bewerber um einen Führerschein nachweisen, dass er nicht nur sein Fahrzeug sicher fahren kann, sondern dass er auch mit dem Inhalt der Straßenverkehrsordnung voll vertraut ist.

P 49 Mehrere bedeutende Projekte sind von österreichischen Unternehmen in Zusammenarbeit mit Firmen anderer Länder ausgeführt worden.

P 50 Selbstverständlich sind die Preise je nach Qualität der Waren unterschiedlich.

P 51 Selbst in unserem sehr fortschrittlichen Zeitalter gibt es Dinge, die jenseits des menschlichen Verstehens liegen. –
Die Scilly Isles liegen jenseits von Land's End, dem südwestlichsten Punkt Englands.

P 52 Der Defekt wurde knapp vor dem Start des Raumschiffes entdeckt.

P 53 Kraft seines Amtes ist der Oberbürgermeister von London der Hauptvertreter der City und ihrer Stadtgemeinde.

P 54 Riesige Dockanlagen erstrecken sich längs des Clyde bei Glasgow.

P 55 Laut Vertrag müssen die Arbeiten bis spätestens Jahresende abgeschlossen sein.

P 56 Der Angeklagte wurde mangels an Beweisen freigesprochen.
Mangels eines besseren Namens nennen wir diese Energieform Reibungselektrizität.

P 57 Zusammen mit Frankreich, der Schweiz, Italien und Spanien gehört Österreich zu den beliebtesten Fremdenverkehrsländern in Europa.

P 46 scenery; unique
P 47 piston
P 48 applicant for, driving licence; to prove; vehicle; contents, the Highway Code
P 49 to carry out
P 51 highly advanced; southwesternmost
P 52 launch; spacecraft, space vessel, space ship
P 53 Lord Mayor [meə]; representative; Corporation
P 54 docks; to extend
P 56 defendant; to acquit; form of energy; frictional electricity
P 57 tourist country

P 58 Schwere Lasten werden mittels Kränen gehoben.

P 59 Die große Westbewegung begann in Amerika nach dem Unabhängigkeitskrieg.

P 60 Er sprach im Namen des Direktors.

P 61 Schloss Windsor neben der Themse ist das größte bewohnte Schloss der Welt.

P 62 Auf den Bergen nennt man die Linie, oberhalb der es keine Bäume gibt, Baumgrenze.

P 63 Der riesige wirtschaftliche Aufschwung in der Welt wäre ohne die bedeutenden Erfindungen und Entdeckungen während der letzten Jahrzehnte unmöglich gewesen.

P 64 Ohne Rücksicht auf die ungünstigen Wetterbedingungen setzten die Forscher ihren Aufstieg fort.

P 65 Oxford ist seit dem 12. Jahrhundert eine Universitätsstadt. –
Seit der Entdeckung Amerikas spielt der neue Kontinent in der Weltwirtschaft eine wichtige Rolle. –
Seit einigen Monaten hat man die Forschung auf diesem Gebiet verstärkt.

P 66 Gab es keinen Einwand seitens der Gewerkschaften?

P 67 An Sonn- und Feiertagen haben die Engländer zu Mittag ein Dinner statt des Lunches und am Abend ein Supper statt des Dinners.

P 68 Teils durch die Besetzung des Landes durch fremde Truppen, teils durch die schweren kriegsbedingten Schäden war das Leben in Österreich in der unmittelbaren Nachkriegsperiode recht schwer.

P 69 Trotz des harten Spiels wurde niemand verletzt. –
Trotz der Spezialisierung, die heutzutage zweifellos notwendig ist, kann der Wert einer guten Allgemeinbildung nicht genug betont werden.

P 70 Heute will ich über die Niagarafälle und den Wellandkanal sprechen. –

P 58 load; to lift; crane
P 59 War of Independence
P 61 to inhabit
P 62 timber line
P 63 boom
P 64 explorer; ascent
P 65 to intensify
P 66 objection; trade(s) unions
P 67 red-letter days
P 68 occupation; troops; damage due to war
P 69 rough play; value; general education
P 70 Welland Canal; grand

Auf seiner Reise quer durch Europa wird mich mein schottischer Freund in Salzburg besuchen. Er wird über Belgien, Deutschland, Österreich, Italien nach Griechenland und in die Türkei fahren. –
Es war für mich ein großartiges Erlebnis, über den Grand Canyon zu fliegen.

P 71 Erst die moderne Weltraumtechnik hat den Menschen befähigt, über die Erdatmosphäre hinauszufliegen.

P 72 Ich kam um etwa 3 Uhr auf dem Londoner Flughafen an.

P 73 Wie jeder weiß, dreht sich die Erde nicht nur um die Sonne, sondern auch um ihre eigene Achse. –
Ein Satellit, der um die Erde kreist, ist ein künstlicher Mond.

P 74 Eine liebende Mutter tut viel mehr um ihrer Kinder willen als um ihrer selbst willen.

P 75 Ungeachtet seiner großen Verluste spielte er weiter.

P 76 Unten am Hochofen wird das geschmolzene Eisen von Zeit zu Zeit abgezogen.

P 77 Unter den Londoner Parkanlagen nimmt der Hydepark eine besondere Stellung ein, da man dort nicht nur Erholung finden, sondern auch an Wochenenden den sogenannten Hydepark-Rednern zuhören kann. –
Die Temperatur fiel bis unter den Gefrierpunkt. –
Ich wählte diese Vase unter den zahlreichen Ausstellungsstücken.

P 78 Plötzlich sah er ein Kind, das unter dem Wrack hervorschaute.

P 79 Die eindrucksvolle Forth Bridge, die den Firth of Forth überspannt, ist nur 7 Meilen von Edinburgh entfernt. –
Amerika ist von vielen Menschen besiedelt worden, die von allen Teilen des Erdballs kamen.

P 80 Warum lief er von zu Hause weg?

P 81 Vor uns sahen wir die Freiheitsstatue und die berühmte Silhouette von New York.

P 82 Auf einer Bootsfahrt auf der Themse von Windsor nach London fuhren wir am Hampton Court Palast vorbei.

P 71 space technology
P 73 an axis, some axes; artificial, man-made
P 76 blast furnace; to draw off
P 77 recreation; speaker, orator; freezing-point; vase [a:]; exhibit [ɪgˈzɪbɪt]
P 78 wreck
P 79 impressive; to span; globe
P 81 skyline

P 83 Der Zweite Weltkrieg ging 1945 zu Ende; sechs Jahre vorher hatte er begonnen.

P 84 Während ihres Aufenthaltes in Wien besuchten meine amerikanischen Freunde mehrere Aufführungen in der Staatsoper. – England war im 17. Jahrhundert während einer Periode von zwölf Jahren eine Republik.

P 85 Wegen des beträchtlichen Interesses musste die Ausstellung verlängert werden. –
Gretna Green, ein kleines schottisches Grenzdorf, ist wegen seiner Schmiede berühmt, in der mehr als 15.000 Ehen von so genannten "run-away couples" geschlossen wurden.

P 86 Wider alle Erwartungen gelang es einem Außenseiter, das Rennen zu gewinnen.

P 87 Wie der Mississippi erreichen alle Gewässer östlich der Rocky Mountains schließlich den Atlantik, während alle Gewässer westlich der Rockies in den Pazifik münden (= fließen).

P 88 Zu jener Zeit war diese Gegend noch unbesiedelt.

P 89 So genannte unbestimmte Zeitadverbien werden im Allgemeinen zwischen den Satzgegenstand und das Zeitwort gesetzt. – Was ist der Unterschied zwischen einem Atom und einem Molekül?

P 83 to come to an end
P 84 to attend a performance; republic [ˈʌ]
P 85 exhibition; to prolong; the Scottish border; a blacksmith's shop; to perform marriages
P 86 expectation; outsider; race
P 87 waters
P 88 uninhabited
P 89 adverb of indefinite time

CONJUNCTIONS AND OTHER CONNECTIVES*

C 1 In Wirklichkeit aber ist die Sache nicht so einfach.
C 2 Allerdings wird diese Arbeit ziemlich schwierig sein.
C 3 Als Kolumbus in Amerika ankam, glaubte er, er sei in Indien gelandet.
C 4 $x^2 = 4$; daher (hence) ist x plus oder minus 2.
C 5 Als die Sonne vom Mond verdeckt wurde, war es, als ob es Nacht wäre.
C 6 Ihr werdet besser spielen müssen; andernfalls werdet ihr verlieren.
C 7 Angenommen, es geschieht; was werdet ihr tun?
C 8 Auch die Engländer haben die Gartenarbeit sehr gerne.
C 9 Er verstand es auch nicht.
C 10 Mir gefällt alles am Lake District, außer dass es in diesem (that) Teil Englands oft regnerisch und wolkig ist.
C 11 In Großbritannien wird alle fünf Jahre eine allgemeine Wahl abgehalten, außer die Regierung erleidet früher eine Niederlage.
C 12 Außerdem gibt es in London mehrere große Parkanlagen.
C 13 Bevor sie in England ankamen, mussten sie eine Landekarte ausfüllen.
C 14 Die beiden berühmtesten englischen Universitätsstädte liegen nordwestlich bzw. nordöstlich von London.
C 15 Er wiederholte das Experiment, bis er Erfolg hatte.
C 16 Wir bedauern, dass wir Sie nicht unterbringen können, da wir für die angegebene Periode ausgebucht sind.
C 17 Da einige ausgezeichnete Impfstoffe vorhanden sind, ist eine Anzahl gefährlicher Krankheiten in unseren Tagen äußerst selten.
C 18 Leider ist das defensive Fahren noch nicht der oberste Grund-

---

* The references are to the conjunctions and other connectives, e.g.: bevor, C 13.
C 1 matters (= things) are
C 4 x squared
C 8 gardening
C 10 cloudy
C 11 to be defeated
C 12 parks
C 13 landing-card, embarkation card; to fill in, to complete (e.g.: a form)
C 16 to accommodate, to put up; the period stated; fully booked
C 17 vaccine ['væksi:n]; disease; rare
C 18 the foremost principle

satz jedes Fahrzeuglenkers. Daher gibt es noch immer so viele Verkehrsunfälle.

C 19 Er benützte ein Mikrofon, damit ihn jeder gut hören konnte.

C 20 Es sind Vorkehrungen getroffen worden, damit diese ansteckende Krankheit nicht auf andere Menschen übertragen wird.

C 21 Zuerst besichtigten wir das Parlamentsgebäude; dann gingen wir in die Westminster Abtei.

C 22 Die Temperatur betrug (= war) 50° F, das sind 10° C.

C 23 Er sagte, es tue ihm Leid, dass er nie in Amerika gewesen sei; er fügte aber hinzu, dass er wahrscheinlich in naher Zukunft nach New York fliegen werde.

C 24 Es besteht sehr große Nachfrage nach Fertigwaren; demgemäß werden immer mehr Fabriken gebaut.

C 25 Wir müssen bis 10 Uhr abends in der Jugendherberge sein, denn Mitgliedern, die später eintreffen, wird der Eintritt verweigert.

C 26 Die Überfahrt war ziemlich rauh; dennoch wurde keiner der Passagiere seekrank.

C 27 Ich konnte es mir nicht leisten, in teuren Hotels zu übernachten; deshalb versuchte ich immer, in Privatpensionen oder Herbergsbetrieben unterzukommen.

C 28 Viele Leute sagten einen Misserfolg voraus; dessen ungeachtet arbeitete George Stephenson an seinem Projekt weiter, bis er 1825 zwischen Stockton und Darlington in Nordengland die erste öffentliche Eisenbahn in Betrieb nahm.

C 29 Zunächst wusste man nicht, was los war; doch einige Minuten später wurde der Schaden entdeckt.

C 30 Er konnte dieses Rätsel ebenfalls lösen.

C 31 Beim Lernen fremder Sprachen ist das Zuhören und Sprechen ebenso wichtig wie das Lesen und Schreiben.

C 32 Ehe ich nach Irland flog, blieb ich einige Tage in London.

C 33 Einerseits ist Oxford eine berühmte Universitätsstadt, andererseits ein wichtiges Industriezentrum.

C 20 to take precautions, to take measures; contagious disease [kən'teɪdʒəs]; to transmit
C 22 centigrade
C 23 to add
C 24 demand; manufactured goods, finished products
C 25 to refuse admission
C 26 passenger
C 27 to afford; to stay at, to put up; private hotel, boarding house; hostel
C 28 to predict; failure; to run a railway (A.: a railroad)
C 29 defect
C 30 riddle, puzzle
C 33 industrial centre

C 34 Ich hätte entweder den Zug oder das Flugzeug benützen können.

C 35 In Edinburgh sagt man, dass Besucher der schottischen Hauptstadt ihres Hafermehlbreis erst würdig sind, wenn sie bis zum Gipfel des Arthur's Seat, der 822 Fuß hoch ist, hinaufgegangen sind.

C 36 Eröffnen Sie ein Bankkonto, falls Sie es vermeiden wollen, große Geldsummen im Haus, Büro oder Geschäft aufzubewahren!

C 37 Ferner enthält der Band einige ausgezeichnete Illustrationen.

C 38 Die Vereinigten Staaten sind ein riesiges Land; folglich ist das Klima in den verschiedenen Teilen der USA sehr unterschiedlich.

C 39 Freilich ist das Ansichtssache.

C 40 Genauso wie der Einzelne von der Gemeinschaft abhängt, hängt die Gemeinschaft vom Einzelnen ab.

C 41 Viele Menschen sprechen nicht nur ihre Muttersprache; sie können sich gleichfalls in wenigstens einer Fremdsprache verständigen.

C 42 Jeder ist gleichsam ein Rädchen in einer großen Maschine.

C 43 Sie verbrachten drei Jahre in Kanada. Danach lebten sie in den Vereinigten Staaten.

C 44 Im Gegenteil, diese Fotos wurden mit einem einfachen Fotoapparat ohne Filter gemacht.

C 45 Immer wenn ich diese Bilder sehe, werde ich an das schottische Hochland (Plural!) erinnert.

C 46 Abfallprodukte, insofern sie für uns schädlich sind, sollten nicht im Freien abgelagert werden.

C 47 An einer Scheune in Südengland las ich folgende Verse, an die ich mich immer gerne erinnere: Eine alte Eule saß auf (in) einer Eiche. Je mehr sie (he) dachte, desto weniger sprach sie; je weniger sie sprach, desto mehr hörte sie. Ich wünschte, alle Leute (folk) wären wie dieser (that) Vogel.

C 35 a visitor to; porridge
C 36 to open a banking account; to keep large sums of money
C 37 volume
C 38 huge; to differ greatly
C 39 a matter of personal approach
C 40 individual; community
C 41 mother tongue; to make oneself understood
C 42 cog
C 44 to take a photo; camera; filter
C 46 waste product; harmful; in the open (air); deposit
C 47 barn; an ancient owl

C 48 Er übersiedelte ins Ausland; drei Monate später kehrte er jedoch wieder nach Hause zurück.

C 49 Je nachdem, ob der Druck vergrößert oder vermindert wird, ist das Volumen des Gases kleiner oder größer.

C 50 Jetzt, da uns so viele Hilfsmittel zur Verfügung stehen, könnten wir uns ein Leben ohne sie nicht mehr vorstellen.

C 51 Kaum hatten wir den Lake District erreicht, standen schwere Wolken am Himmel.

C 52 Ich verstand den Text erst, nachdem ich ihn einige Male gelesen hatte.

C 53 Die Verslehre unterscheidet vier wichtige Versfüße, nämlich den Jambus, den Trochäus, den Anapäst und den Daktylus.

C 54 Natürlich musste man einen Kanal, den so genannten Wellandkanal, zwischen Ontario- und Eriesee bauen, um die Niagarafälle zu umgehen.

C 55 Nicht einmal die Probleme der Schwerelosigkeit konnten den Menschen daran hindern, in den Weltraum einzudringen.

C 56 Englands höchster Berg, Scafell Pike, ist nicht so hoch wie der höchste Gipfel von Wales, Snowdon.

C 57 Barclays Bank ist nicht nur in den meisten Städten Großbritanniens, sondern auch in vielen Teilen des Commonwealth und in einigen fremden Ländern vertreten.

C 58 Die Qualität der Radio- und Fernsehgeräte ist ausgezeichnet; nichtsdestoweniger versuchen Radiotechniker, sie wenn möglich zu verbessern.

C 59 Obwohl bereits beträchtliche Fortschritte auf diesem Gebiet erzielt worden sind, muss noch eine Menge getan werden.

C 60 Wir wissen noch immer nicht, wann das möglich sein wird.

C 61 Noch nie genossen so viele Menschen einen so hohen Lebensstandard.

C 62 Wir wissen noch nicht, ob sich diese Vorhersagen bewahrheiten werden.

C 48 to move
C 49 pressure; increase, reduce
C 50 facilities; to be available
C 53 in English prosody there are; iambus [aɪ'æmbəs]; trochee ['trəuki:]; anapaest ['ænəpi:st]; dactyl ['dæktɪl]; foot
C 54 Welland Canal; to avoid
C 55 weightlessness ['weɪt-]; to prevent from -ing
C 56 peak, top, summit; Scafell [,skɔ:'fel]
C 57 to represent
C 58 radio engineer
C 59 to achieve
C 62 prediction; to come true

C 63 Nur auf diese Weise wird es möglich sein, die Lebensbedingungen in den Entwicklungsländern zu verbessern. (Inversion nach only am Satzanfang!)
C 64 Wo man seine Ferien verbringt, hängt davon ab, ob man das Gebirge oder das Meer bevorzugt.
C 65 Obwohl das Buch in erster Linie für Schüler und Studenten geschrieben worden ist, kann es mit Nutzen von jedem verwendet werden, der sich für die englische Sprache interessiert.
C 66 Bevorzugen Sie, das Spiel im Stadion oder auf dem Fernsehschirm zusehen?
C 67 Seit die Atomenergie entdeckt wurde, lebt der Mensch nicht nur voller Erwartungen, sondern auch in Angst.
C 68 Ich habe ihn seither nicht gesehen.
C 69 Selbst wenn die Sicht schlecht ist, können dort Flugzeuge auf Grund einer automatischen Landeanlage sicher landen.
C 70 So werden im ganzen Lande große Kraftwerke zur Erzeugung von Elektrizität gebaut.
C 71 Sie werden uns informieren, sobald sie es selbst wissen.
C 72 Sobald der Satellit in den Weltraum geschickt worden ist, gerät er in eine elliptische Erdumlaufbahn.
C 73 Er sprach langsam und deutlich, sodass wir ihm leicht folgen konnten.
C 74 Sofern wir genug Geld und Zeit haben, wollen wir auch der pazifischen Küste einen Besuch abstatten.
C 75 Sogar gut ausgerüstete Bergsteiger müssen sehr vorsichtig sein.
C 76 Solange er in Schottland arbeitet, wird er bei seinem schottischen Freund wohnen.
C 77 Wir werden nicht mit dem Zug, sondern mit dem Flugzeug reisen.
C 78 Ihr müsst mehr studieren, sonst werdet ihr die Sprache nicht gut sprechen können.
C 79 Sooft ich in London war, besuchte ich eine Aufführung in einem der berühmten Westend-Theater.
C 80 Versuchen Sie, so schnell wie möglich zu übersetzen!

C 65 primarily; with profit
C 66 stadium; television screen
C 67 expectation
C 69 visibility; poor; landing system
C 70 power station; to generate electricity
C 72 to go into orbit
C 74 to pay a visit to
C 75 to equip; a mountaineer

C 81 Einige englische Privatpensionen bieten nur Zimmer mit Frühstück an, andere Zimmer, Frühstück sowie Abendessen.

C 82 Sowohl in Wales als auch in Schottland gibt es Nationalisten, die fordern, dass die Waliser bzw. die Schotten als völlig verschiedene Nationen anerkannt werden.

C 83 Derzeit sind wir sozusagen erst an der Schwelle der riesigen kosmischen Räume.

C 84 Teils war es wolkig und regnerisch, teils gab es Sonnenschein.

C 85 Er wurde verletzt; trotzdem spielte er weiter.

C 86 Überdies sollten wir nicht vergessen (= wir uns daran erinnern), dass das Geld sicher ist, sobald es in eine Bank eingezahlt ist.

C 87 Übrigens gibt es zwei Lösungen.

C 88 Bevor wir die Eishöhle betraten, zogen wir den Pullover an, um uns nicht zu erkälten.

C 89 Sie wird einige Monate in Frankreich verbringen, um ihre Französischkenntnisse zu verbessern.

C 90 Alle Zimmer in den angeführten Hotels haben privates Bad, Farbfernsehen, Radio und Telefon mit direkter Durchwahl.

C 91 Gleichgültig ob man viel Geld hat oder nicht, kann man dort einen wunderbaren Urlaub machen.

C 92 Die meisten Firmen bieten freie Stellen unter der Bedingung an, dass die Bewerber Referenzen angeben.

C 93 Das ist vielmehr eine Frage des persönlichen Geschmacks.

C 94 Vor allem möchte ich zwei Dinge erwähnen.

C 95 Ich will Ihnen darüber einen kurzen Bericht geben, vorausgesetzt, dass Sie sich dafür interessieren.

C 96 Während sich unser Schiff Dover näherte, sahen wir das Schloss auf den weißen Kreidefelsen.

C 97 Üben Sie das Sprechen von Fremdsprachen, wann immer es möglich ist.

C 98 Ich wurde nach Kanada geschickt, was genau das war, was ich wollte.

C 99 Was auch immer geschehen mag, eines (= ein Ding) ist sicher:...

C 81 Note: To avoid ambiguity, proprietors of private hotels (= boarding houses) usually refer to dinner as "evening dinner"
C 82 to claim; entirely different; to recognise as
C 83 threshold; space
C 86 to pay into
C 88 ice-cave; to catch cold
C 90 the hotels listed; direct dial telephone
C 92 vacancy; applicant; to furnish references
C 96 to approach
C 97 to practise (A.: to practice)

C 100 Weder ihm noch seinem Freund gelang es, das Kreuzworträtsel zu lösen.

C 101 Die französische, italienische, spanische, portugiesische und rumänische Sprache (Plural!) haben viele Wörter gemeinsam, weil sie alle vom Lateinischen hergeleitet sind.

C 102 Weiterhin muss bedacht werden, dass der Lufttransport viel teurer als der Wassertransport ist.

C 103 Informationen (Singular!) über den Charakter und die Fähigkeiten einer Person tragen meist den Titel: Wen immer es betreffen mag.

C 104 Wenn wir das Flugzeug benützt hätten, hätten wir viel Zeit gespart.

C 105 Wenn das Internet auch eine Fülle an Informationen bietet, so sollte man doch nicht die Printmedien außer Acht lassen.

C 106 Wenn nicht anders angegeben, schließen die angeführten Preise für Einzelzimmer das Frühstück sowie alle Abgaben ein.

C 107 Wer auch immer es versuchen mag, er wird keinen Erfolg haben.

C 108 Wie ein englischer Dichter gesagt hat, haben die Engländer „ein grünes und angenehmes Land".

C 109 Wo es möglich ist, ist es ratsam, Vorausbestellungen durchzuführen.

C 110 Bei diesen Versuchen wird bewiesen, dass ungleiche elektrische Ladungen einander anziehen, wogegen gleiche Ladungen einander abstoßen.

C 111 Niemand wusste, woher er gekommen war.

C 112 Er sagte nicht, wohin er geht.

C 113 Wo immer du bist, denke daran, dass du Vertreter deines Vaterlandes bist!

C 114 Er machte eine garstige Bemerkung, worauf sie das Zimmer verließ.

C 115 Wir haben verschiedene Werkzeuge; z. B.: Hämmer, Schraubenzieher, Feilen.

C 116 Zwar sind beim Lernen fremder Sprachen audiovisuelle Hilfsmittel von großer Bedeutung; sie können aber nicht alle herkömmlichen Lehr- und Lernmethoden ersetzen.

C 100 crossword puzzle
C 101 in common; to derive
C 102 to take into consideration, to take into account
C 103 to bear the title; to concern
C 105 print media
C 106 otherwise stated; the prices quoted; single bedroom; charges
C 109 advisable; to make advance reservations
C 110 (un)like charges; to attract; to repel
C 113 a representative; native country
C 114 nasty
C 115 screwdriver, file
C 116 audio-visual aids; traditional

INDEX

English Part*

above, 38
accelerate, 125
accomplish a task, 173
account, 32; – for, 85
    to take into –, 31
    on no –, 70
achieve, 6
achievement, 16
acquainted with, 20, 26
active, to play an – part, 23
actually, 66, 82
adage 36
add, 42, 43, 77 – to, 125
address, 1
admit, 62, 76
adopt, 17, 133, 134
advance, 6, 12
advantage, 141, 168
affect, 123
afterwards, 162
age, 2
ago, not too long –, 156
agree, 56
ahead, to look –, 172
aim, 34, 127
all, above –, 48
    all in all, 167
allow, 125
amazing, 28, 120
among, to be –, 11, 15
ancient, 155
anyway, 69, 78
apparatus, 17
apparent, 58, 59
appear, 60, 68
appliance, 17
application, 17
apply, 17, 133, 134
    – to, 80, 81
appreciate, 11, 26
approach, 31, 142
argue, 37
argument, 35
arrange, 139
arise, 142
    the question arises, 87
arrive at the conclusion, 168
art, 147
article, 35
artistic, 15
as it were, 105
associated with, 21
association, 21
assume, 37, 74
astonishing, 120
astounding, 28
attach importance to, 94
attention, 29, 44, 95
available, 144
avoid, 126
aware, to be –, 31, 56

based upon, 19
basic(ally), 22
bear on, 123
bear in mind, 26, 31
bearing, 123
beauty spot, 13
before, 38
    – that time, 165
begin, 29, 150
beginning, 29, 149
behalf, on – of, 1
belief, 36
believe, 3, 68, 78, 79, 167, 172
    ... is believed to, 11, 75
below, 38
beneficial, 130
best, it would be – to, 167
birth, to give – to, 128
book, 35
bound up with, 21
brief, 43, 106
bring about, 96, 128
broadly (speaking), 102
brochure, 35

call, 8, 104
captivating, 28
care, 95
career, 47
careful, 68
carry, this would – me too far, 46
carry out experiments, 7
case, 61, 112, 116
    in any –, 69
    in no –, 70
category, 139
cause, 96, 128
centre, 15
centred upon, 19
century 37, 149, 150, 151, 152, 154
certain, 56, 172
    to know for –, 67
chairman, 1
change, 6

* The references are to the patterns (1–175); e.g.: different from, 137

characterise, 122
characteristic, 11, 121
chief, 22
circumstance, 108, 110
cite, 45, 48
city, 13
class 18, 139
classify, 139
clear, the following
becomes –, 68
close, the – of the
century, 149
to draw to a –, 150
closely connected, 21
come, – across, 28
– back to, 44
– to an end, 150
– up to expectations, 132
compare, 131, 147
comparison, by –, 48
comparatively speaking,
102
composed, to be – of, 22
composition, 32, 171
comprise, 140
concentrate, 53
concern, 54
– oneself with, 32
concerned with, 39
conclude, 74, 166, 168
conclusion, 166, 168, 169
condition, 109, 166
confess, 76
confine oneself, 53
connected with, 21
connection, 21, 29
conscious, to be – of, 31
consider, 29, 31, 45, 119,
141, 167, 168
... is considered to, 11,
75
considerable, 123, 129,
137
consideration, 31, 68, 95
consist of, 22
constitute, 12
contain, 35
contents, 35
context, 29
contrary, 82
contrast, 137, 138, 147
contribute, 129
contribution, 129
controversy, 87
conversant with, 20, 26
converse, the – is true, 82
convinced, 3, 56
cope with, 132
corner-stone, 16
correct, 167
correspond to, 136
course, 161
cover, 140
– a period, 35
– a wide field, 35
create, 96
cultural, 15
current, 154
customary, 116

daring, 28
date from, 151
day, in his days, 155
deal with, 9, 29, 35, 38,
39, 41, 142
decade, 6, 150
decisive, 28
decrease, 126
define, 8, 29
degree, 115
delighted, 99
demand, 132
demonstrate, 9, 38
denote, 55, 103
deny, 62, 63
depend upon, 19
describe, 8, 9, 29, 38
description, 32, 145
designed for, 17
detail, 31, 46
determine, 123
development, 6
device, 17
differ from, 137
difference, 135
different from, 137
differentiate, 138
difficult, 3, 79
difficulty, 142
directly proportional, 136
disadvantage, 141
discard, 134
disclose, 9
discuss, 31
dislike, 146
disposal, at one's –, 144
dispute, 76
disregard, 51
distinction, 138
distinguish, 138
divide, 139
do, 127, 129
domestic appliance, 17
doubt, 63
beyond –, without –,
no –, 64
doubtful, 65
doubtless, 65
draw a person's attention
to, 29, 44
drawback, 141, 168
drop a subject, 46
due to, 19, 84
dwell upon a subject, 46

earlier, 38
easy, 124, 131
economic, 15
effect, 123
effort, 6
eliminate, 126, 127
embark on, 31
emergency, in an –, 114
emphasis, 95
emphasise, 166
emphatic(ally), 166
employ, 17, 133, 134
enable, 124
encounter, 142
end, 149
to come to an –, 150

in the –, 162, 166
endeavour, 171
engineering feat, 16
enhance, 125
enjoy, 3
ensure, 124
equal, to be – to, 136
without –, 131
era, 2, 150
essential, 11, 22, 23, 91, 135
esteem, 11
event, 15
in any –, 69
at all events, 69
eventually, 96, 162, 167
ever–increasing, 115
every now and then, 159
everything else, like –, 141
evident, 58, 59, 61
exaggerate, 94
examination, on closer –, 68
examine, 44
example, 45, 48, 49, 50, 52, 53
exception, 51, 52
exciting, 28
exclusive, 86
exert an influence on, 123
exigency, 132
expect, 73, 116, 167, 172
... is expected to, 75
expectation, 132
experience, 57
experiment, 7
explain, 29, 38, 85
exploit, 133
extend back to, 151
extend a welcome, 1
extent, 115
extraordinary, 28
extensively used, 133
extremely useful, 130

face difficulties, 142
facilitate, 124
facility, 144
fact, 66, 82, 85
factor, 31
fall into, 139
familiar with, 20
familiarise oneself with, 26
famous, 11, 13
fascinating, 28
favour, 24, 125
in – of, 90
favourable, 109, 131
feat, 16
feature, 47
feel, 71, 77, 167
feeling, 72
field, 6, 7, 12, 35, 133
figurative, 103
finally, 162
fine, 11
first, at –, 162
the – to, 9
– of all, 29, 30, 141, 162
follow, as follows, 35, 139
following, 139
forefront, to come into the –, 24
forget, 40
former, in – times, 37, 155
formerly, 37, 155
fortnight, a –, 15 6
fortunately, 99
founded on, 19
frank, 79
frequent, 116, 133
frequently visited, 13
function, 34
fundamental, 135
further, 42, 43, 125
future, 172, 175

gadget, 17
gain popularity, 24
gather from, 27
general, in –, 102
generally speaking, 102
genius, 148
gentlemen, 1
give, – an example, 45, 49
– birth to, 128
– consideration, 95
– rise to, 96, 128
glad, 99
glance, at first –, 68
go as far back as, 151
grade, 139
granted, to take for –, 37
great, 1, 11, 15, 16
greatly, 129
greatness, 148
ground, to gain –, 24
group, 18, 139

happen, 28, 116, 172
happy, I am – to say that, 99
hardly, 62
head(ing), 55, 139
hear, 28
heavens, thank –, 82, 99
help, I cannot – thinking, 77
hesitate, 79
highlight, 16, 47
historic, 12
historically speaking, 102
hold, – a place, 10
– (true) for, 80
whatever the future may –, 172
holiday resort, 13
honour, 1
hope, 166, 172
household (= domestic) appliance, 17
household gadget, 17

idea, 26, 29
identical, 136
ignore, 94
illustrate, 45, 49
imagine, 3, 4, 79

immediate, 153
impact, 123
impair, 123
imply, 55
importance, 25, 91, 94
important, 11, 15, 16, 23, 91, 129, 135
impossible 98, 124
impression, 72
improbable, 60
improve, 124
improvement, 6, 12
inclined to agree, 56
include, 140
incompatible with, 89
inconsistent with, 89
increase, 115, 125, 127, 132
incredible, 83, 120
indicate, 38
indication, 5, 166
indispensable, 93
induce, 128
industrial, 15
inestimable, 17
inevitable, 96
influence, 123
influential, 11
ingenious, 16
innovation, 12
inseparable, 21
inspection, on more careful –, 68
installation, 17
instance, 48, 50
instrument, 17
intended for, 17
interested in, 3, 119
interesting to note, 119
interval, at intervals, 159
intimately linked, 21
introduce, 1, 134
invention, 19
inversely proportional, 137
investigation, 7
irreconcilable, 89
judge, 26
judging from (by), 74

key, 85
kind, 18
kitchen utensil, 17
know, 26, 57, 67, 172
knowledge, 19
known (as), 11
    best –, 13, 15

landmark, 16
large(ly), 22, 84, 86, 133
last, at –, 162
    – of all 162
lately, 6
later, 38, 162
lay emphasis on, 95
lead to, 96, 128
leading, 23
learn, 27
leave aside, 44
lecture, 32
legend, 36
length, at – , 162
lie, 14
life, 4, 47
like, there is nothing –, 131
likely, 60
limitation, 141
linked (up) with, 21
literal, 103
literary, 15
located, 14
long, not too – ago, 156
    in the – run, 161, 162
look, – closely, 68
    – further ahead, 172
    – upon as, 11
love, 146
lucky, 99

machine, 17
made, to be – up of, 22
magazine, 27, 35
main, 22, 86
maintain, 3, 10
major, a – part, 23
make easier, 124
master, 147
masterpiece, 145
match, nothing can – with, 131
matter, 68, 86, 91, 92
    – of fact, 66, 82
    to go to the root of the –, 68
may, be it as it –, 172
mean, 30, 103, 117
meaning, 103
means, 18
    by all –, 69
    by no –, 70
    by this –, 173
meantime, in the –, 158
meanwhile, 158
meet with problems, 142
meet the requirements, 132
memorable, 28
mention, 29, 38, 40, 41, 48, 77, 119, 141
mere, 86
method, 16, 18, 134
mid-century, by –, 149
middle, in the – of, 149
mind, to bear in –, 26, 31
    to my –, 71
mirror, 145, 146
mistake, 94
modern, 11
moment, at the –, 160
music(al), 15

name, 55, 148
natural, 58
necessary, 93, 124
necessitate, 124
necessity, 25
need, 25, 63, 128, 132
neglect, 94
newspaper, 27
notable, 6, 11
note, 42, 119

noteworthy, 119
nothing, there is
– like, 131
now, every – and then, 159
till –, 163
nowadays, 154
numerous, 18
nutshell, to put it in a –,
106

object, 34, 127
obtain, 6
obvious, 58, 39
occasion, 111
occur, 6
off, situated –, 14
offer, 141
only, the – one to, 9
opinion, 3, 71, 72
opposite, 82
order, in – to, 127
original meaning, 103
other, among – things, 48
the – day, the – morning, the – night, 156
outcome, 172
outset, at the –, 29
outstanding, 10, 11, 15,
129
overcome, 142
overestimate, 94
overlook, 94
overrate, 94
overstress, 25
overvalue, 94
owe to, 19

paramount, 23
part, to play a –, 23
I, for my –, 71
particular, 84, 110, 130
partly, 84
past, in the, 155
pay attention to, 95
pay tribute to, 174
peculiar, 121
period, 35, 150, 153
permit, 125
persuaded, I am – of 78
perusal, at first –, 68
pity, what a –, 10 1
place, 10, 13
play a part, 23
pleased, 99
pleasure, 1
plot, 35
point, 87
point out, 29, 38, 62, 63,
166
point of view, 113
political, 15
popular, 11, 13, 24
popularity, 24
position, 10
positive, 56
possess, 141
possibility, 175
possible, 124, 173
post-war period, 153
predilection, 146
predominant, 10, 86
pre-eminent, 129
preference, 146
present, at – 5, 154, 160
presumable, 59
presume, 73
... is presumed to, 75
prevent, 126
previously, 38, 44, 155, 165
pre-war years, 153
primarily, 22, 32, 35, 86
primary object, 34
principal, 22
privilege, 1
probability, 59
probable, 59, 60, 84
problem, 43, 85, 142
process, 18, 134
progress, 6
proof, 45, 88
promote, 125
proportional, directly –,
136
inversely –, 137
pros and cons, 168
prove, 9, 17, 38, 52, 88,
130, 146, 171
proverb, 36
provide (for), 144
pure, 86
purpose, 17, 34, 110, 127
put, to – it in a nutshell,
106
to – it differently, 107

queer, 28
question, 44, 86, 87
quote, 48

raise, 125
– the question, 87
rank, 10
rate, at any –, 69
rather, 86
reach the conclusion, 168
read, 28
realise, 25, 31 119
reason, 49, 170, 172
it stands to –, 62
recall, 29
recent, 6, 156
recognise, 9
recreational area, 13
reduce, 126, 127
refer to, 38, 39, 41, 48, 54
reflect, 145
reflection, on –, 68
regard as, 11
regret, 101
regrettable, 101
reign, 155
related field, 133
relate to, 54
religious, 15
remain, 43
remark, 42, 53
remarkable, 12, 15, 28,
115
remember, 26, 31, 119,
148, 166
remind a person of, 29

renowned, 11, 13
repeat, 166
report, 27
representative, 11
reputed to be, 11
requirement, 132
resemble, 136
resist, I cannot – stating, 77
resort, 13
respects, in some –, 113
rest upon, 19
restrict oneself to, 53
result, 6
  – in, 96, 128
reveal, 9, 145, 146
rid, to get – of, 143
rise, to give – to, 96, 128
role, 23
root, to go to the – of, 68
roughly, 102, 136
rule, 52
run, in the long –, 161, 162

safe, it seems – to say, 167
same, the – as, 13 6
say, 41, 62, 90, 166, 167
  that is to –, 107
  this is not to – that, 117
  the same may be said of, 118
  is said to, 75
saying, 36
  it goes without –, 62
scale, on a large –, 7
scarcely, 62
scholastic, 15
scientific, 15
see, 38, 147, 169
seem, 60, 68, 72, 78, 83, 97, 167
sense, 103, 104
serve, 17
several, 18
short, in –, 106
show, 9, 38, 145, 146
sight, 13
  at first –, 68
significance, 91, 94
similar, 111, 136
similarity, 135
simple, 124
simplify, 124
simply and solely, 86
simultaneous, 157
situated, 14
so-called, 104
so far, 163
solve, 9, 142
sorry, I am – to say that, 100
sort, 18
sound, 83
spa, 13
speak, 1
speak, so to –, 105
speaking, strictly –, 102
sporting, 15
spot, 13
start, to – with, 29
startling, 120
state, 38, 77, 170
statement, 27
step, 12
store, to lie in –, 172
story, 36
strange, 28, 78
stress, 95
striking, 120, 135
study, after careful –, 68
subdivide, 139
subject, 31, 33, 46
subsequently, 162
success, 6
successful, 133
suffer from, 141
suggest, 55
sum up, 139, 166
summarise, 166
summary, 32
supply the key to, 85
suppose, 73, 74
  … is supposed to, 75
sure, 56
surprising, 58, 120
survey, 32

tackle, 142
take care, 95
take for granted, 37
talk, 32, 171
task, 34, 173
taste, 71, 146
technique, 134
tell, 62
tend, 68
tendency, 5
term, 8
thank heavens, 82, 99
theme, 33
then, 162, 164
  before –, 165
  every now and –. 159
thing, all things considered, 167
think, 3, 77, 167
thorough, 35
thought, 3
  on second thoughts, 68
threshold, 2
thrilling, 28
thus, 169
till now, 163
time, 2, 164, 165
  at the same –, 157
  for the – being, 160
  from – to –, 159
  in his –, 155
  in the course of –, 161
  in ancient times, 155
  in former times, 155
title, 55
topic, 33
trace as far back as, 151
tradition, 36
trend, 5
tribute, to offer –, to pay –, 174
true, 80, 81, 82, 83, 97

truth, 78
turn, the – of the century, 149
turn to, 44, 45
turning-point, 16
type, 18, 141
typical, 11, 121

ultimately, 162
unbelievable, 120
uncertain(ty), 65
underestimate, 94
underplot, 35
underrate, 94
understand, 26
undertake investigations, 7
undervalue, 94
undoubted, 64
unequalled, 131
unfavourable, 131
unfortunate, 100, 101
unimaginable, 4
universal, 17, 133
unknown, 65
unlikely, 60
unmatched, 131
unnecessary, 124
unparalleled, 131
unpredictable, 172
unrivalled, 131
unsurpassed, 131
until now, 163
unusual, 28
up-to-date, 11
up to now, 163
use, 17, 103, 133, 134
useful, 130
useless, 98
usual, 116
utilise, 133
utmost, 91

valuable, 12, 129, 130
value, 17
variety, 18, 139
various, 18
versatile, 11
view, on a closer –, 68
in my –, 71
with a – to, 127
viewpoint, 31, 113
visit, 13
vital, 23
volume, 35

watering-place, 13
way, in this –, 173
by the –, 40
ways (of), 18, 113, 139
week, 156
weigh the pros and cons, 168
welcome, 1
well, it may – be that, 97
it may be – to repeat, 166
while, after a –, 162
whole, on the –, 167
widespread, 17, 133
witness, 28
wonder, 67
word, 118
in a –, 106
in other words, 107
work(s), 145, 146, 147
world war, 153
worse, 124
worst, if the – comes to the –, 114
worth considering, 119

year, 153

GERMAN PART*

abhängen, 19
Abneigung, 146
abschließend, 166
Abschluss, 166
abschneiden, (un)günstig –, 131
Absicht, 127
abstreiten, 62, 63, 76
abwägen, 168
achten auf, 95
ähneln, 136
ähnlich, 111, 136
Ähnlichkeit, 135
Ahnung, 26, 29
aktiv, 23
aktuell, 66 Fußnote
alles andere, wie –, 141
alles in allem, 167
allgemein, 102, 103, 133
allgemein verwendet, 17, 133
alt, in alten Zeiten, 155
anders als, 137
unter anderem, 48
andeuten, 38, 55
Anerkennung zollen, 174
Anfang, 29, 149
anfangen, 29, 150
Anforderung, 132
anführen, Beispiele –, 45, 48, 49
angeben, 38, 170
angeblich, 75
angedeihen lassen, Sorgfalt –, 95
Angelegenheit, 68, 86
ankommen, auf etwas –, 91, 92
Anlage, 17
Annahme, zur – neigen, 3, 68
es besteht Grund zur –, 172
annehmen, 37, 73, 74
anordnen, 139
anpacken, 142
anreden, 1
ansehen als, 11
Ansicht, 71
ansprechen, 1
anstellen, Versuche –, 7
Anstrengung, 6
antreffen, 28, 142
anwenden, 17, 133, 134
Anzeichen, 5, 166
Apparat, 17
Art, 18, 139
Artikel, 35
auffallend, 120, 135
Aufgabe, 3, 4, 173
aufgeben, 134
Autmerksamkeit, 29, 44, 95
aufnehmen, es – mit, 131
aufregend, 28
Aufsatz, 42, 171
Aufsehen erregend, 120
auftreten, 6, 142
Auftrieb verleihen, 96, 128
aufwerfen, eine Frage –, 87
Augenblick, 160
augenscheinlich, 58, 59
ausdrücken, 55, 107
ausführen, 29, 38
auslaufend, 152
Ausnahme, 51, 52
ausnützen, 133
ausschalten, 126, 127
ausschließlich, 86
aussehen, 83
außergewöhnlich, 28
äußerst, 91, 130
ausüben, einen Einfluss –, 123
auszeichnen, sich – durch, 122
Auszeichnung, 1
Badeort, 13
Band, 35
beabsichtigt, 17
beachten, 31, 94, 95
beachtenswert, 119
Beachtung, 95
Bedarf, 132
bedauerlich, 101
bedauern, 101
bedenken, 26, 31, 119
bedeuten, 103, 117
bedeutend, 11, 15, 16, 23, 91, 92, 129, 135
Bedeutung, 25, 91, 94, 103
Bedingung, 109, 166
Bedürfnis, 128, 132
beeinflussen, 123
beeinträchtigen, 123
befähigen, 124
beginnen, 29, 150
begründet, 19
begrüßen, 1
begünstigen, 125
behandeln, 9, 29, 32, 35, 38, 39, 41
behaupten, 3, 37
Stellung–, 10
beibehalten, 10
beimessen, Bedeutung 94
Wert –, 95
beinhalten, 35
beiseite lassen, 44
Beispiel, 45, 48, 49, 50, 52, 53
Beitrag, beitragen, 129
beiwohnen, 28
bekannt, 11, 13, 15, 20, 26, 148
– werden, 26
beleuchten, 45, 49
beliebt, 11, 13, 24
Beliebtheit, 24
bemerkenswert, 6, 11, 115, 28, 115, 119

* The references are to the patterns (1 – 175)–, e.g.: anders als 137.

Bemerkung, 42, 43, 53
bemühen, sich –, 171
bereit, 76
Bericht, 27, 32
berücksichtigen, 29, 31, 95, 167, 168
beruhen auf, 19, 148
berühmt, 11, 13
beschäftigen, sich – mit, 32, 39
beschleunigen, 125
beschränken, sich – auf, 53
beschreiben, 8, 9, 29, 38
Beschreibung, 32, 145
bestehen aus, 22
bestimmen, 123
bestimmt für, 1
bestreiten, 76
besuchen, 13
betonen, 25, 95, 166
Betracht, in – ziehen, 31, 51
betrachten, 29, 45, 141
betrachtet werden als, 1
beträchtlich, 123, 129, 137
betreffen, 54, 123
betreiben, Forschungen –, 7
beweisen, 9, 38, 52, 88 146, 171
bewusst sein, 31, 56
bezeichnen, 8, 55, 103
beziehen, sich – auf, 38 39, 41, 54
bieten, 141, 144
bisher, bis jetzt, 163
bleiben, 43, 46
Blick, auf den ersten –, 68
blicken, in die Zukunft –, 172
Boden, an – gewinnen, 24
bringen, mit sich -, 96, 128
    was immer die Zukunft – mag, 172
Broschüre, 35
Buch, 35

charakterisieren, 122
charakteristisch, 11, 121
    –es Merkmal, 47

damals, 164
Damen und Herren, 1
Dank, Gott sei –, 82, 99
dann, 162
darstellen, 12, 38
dartun, 9, 29, 38
decken, den Bedarf –, 132
definieren, 8, 29
demonstrieren, 9, 38
denken, 77, 167
    wenig an –, 3
denkwürdig, 28
derzeit, 160
Detail, 31, 46
deutlich, 61
dienen zu, 17
diskutieren, 31
durchlesen, Durchsicht, 68

echt (= charakteristisch), 11
eher, 86
Ehre, 1
eigenartig, 28
Eindruck, 72
eindrucksvoll, 28
einfach 86, 124
Einfluss 123
einflussreich, 11
einführen, 134
eingehen auf, 31, 39
einnehmen, Stellung unter –, 10
einschätzen, 26
einschließen, 140
einteilen, 139
Einwirkung, 123
Einzelheit, 31, 46
Einzige, der –, 9
eliminieren, 126, 127
Ende, 149 am
    –, 162, 166
    zu – gehen, 150
Endergebnis, 172
endlich, 162
eng verbunden, 21
enthalten, 35
enthüllen, 9, 145, 146
entnehmen, 27
entscheidend, 28
entsprechen, 136
    den Erfordernissen –, 132
    den Erwartungen –, 132
Entwicklung, 6
ereignen, sich –, 28, 116, 172
Ereignis, 15
erfahren, 27
Erfahrung, 57
Erfindung, 19
Erfolg, 6
erfolgreich, 133
Erfordernis, 132
erfreut, 99
erfüllen, die Aufgabe –, 173
ergeben, 96, 128
    es ergibt sich Folgendes 68
Ergebnis, 6
erheben, es erhebt sich die Frage, 87
erhöhen, 125, 127
Erholungsgebiet, 13
erinnern, 26, 29, 31, 119, 148, 166
erkennen, 9, 25, 31, 119
erklären, 29, 38, 77, 85
Erklärung, 27
erlauben, 125
erläutern, 38, 45, 49
erleichtern, 124
erregend, 28

erreichen, 6
Errungenschaft, 16
erscheinen, 60
ersehen aus, 147
erstaunlich, 28, 120
Erste, der –, 9
auf den ersten Blick, 68
in erster Linie, 22, 32, 35, 86
erwägen, 31, 51, 119, 168
erwähnen, 29, 38, 40, 41, 48, 77, 141
erwähnenswert, 119
erwarten, 73, 116, 167, 172
Erwartung, 132
erweisen, sich –, 17, 130
erwiesen, als – annehmen, 37
erzielen, Fortschritte –, 6
Experiment, 7

Faktor, 31
Fall, 50, 61, 112, 116
auf alle Fälle, 69
auf keinen –, 70
der – sein, 61
fallen lassen, Thema –, 46
Fehler, 94
Ferienort, 13
fertig werden mit, 142
fesselnd, 28
feststellen, 38, 62, 63, 77
Folge, zur – haben, 96, 128
folgen, wie folgt, 35, 139
fördern, 125
Forschung, 7
Fortschritt, 6, 12
Frage, 44, 86, 87
freilich, 97
Freude, 1
freuen, 99
früher, 37, 38, 44, 155, 165
Für, das – und Wider, 168
führen zu, 96, 128
zu weit führen, 46
führend, 23

geben, Beispiele –, 45, 49
Gebiet, 6, 7, 12, 35, 133
verwandtes –, 133
Gebrauch, 17, 103
gebrauchen, 17, 133, 134
gebührend, 95
Gedanken, sich – machen, 3
Gefühl, 72
Gegensatz, 137
Gegenstand, 33
Gegenteil, 82
gegenüber, sich – sehen, 142
gegenüberstellen, 138, 147
gegenwärtig, 154, 160
gehen, zu Ende –, 150
nichts geht über, 131
gehören zu, 11, 15, 140
Gelegenheit, 111
gelten als, 11
das gilt für, 80, 81
genauer ausdrücken, 107
genauer hinsehen, 68
genau genommen, 102
geneigt, 56
genial, 16
Genie, 148
genießen, 3
Gerät, 17
geringer, 115
geschehen, 28, 116, 172
Geschichte, 36
Geschmack, 71, 146
Gesichtspunkt, 31, 113
gestatten, 125
gestehen, 76
gewährleisten, 124
gewinnen, an Beliebtheit –, an Boden –, 24
gewiss, in gewissem Sinne, 104
gewöhnlich, 116
Glaube, 36
glauben, 3, 68, 71, 77, 78, 79, 167, 172
man könnte –, 68
gleich, 136
gleichkommen, 131
gleichsam, 105
gleichzeitig, 157
glücklicherweise, 99
Gott, – sei Dank, 82, 99
Grad, 115
grob, 102, 136
groß, in –em (Umfang), 7
im Großen und Ganzen, 167
Größe, 148
Großtat, 16
Grund, 49
der Sache auf den – gehen, 68
es besteht – zur Annahme, 172
aus den angegebenen Gründen, 170
grundlegend, 135
gründlich, 35
Grundstein, 16
Gruppe, 18, 139
gruppieren, 139
günstig, 109, 131
gut, es wäre –, 166

handeln von, 35
Handlung, 35
häufig, 116, 133
häufig besucht, 13
hauptsächlich, 22, 8, 4, 86
Hauptzweck, 34
Haushaltsgerät, 17
heben, 125
heißen, das heißt, 107, 117
herabsetzen, 126, 127
herangehen an, 31, 142
hernach, 162

Herren, 1
hervorragend, 10, 11, 15, 23, 129
heutzutage, 154
Hilfsmittel, 144
hindern, 126
Hinsicht, 113
hinweisen, 29, 38, 41, 48, 62, 63, 166
hinzufügen, 42, 43, 77
historisch, 12, 102
hoch erfreut, 99
Höchstleistung, 16
höchstwahrscheinlich, 60
hoffen, 166, 172
Höhe, auf der – von, 14
Höhepunkt, 16, 47
hören, 28

identisch, 136
illustrieren, 45, 49
immer, sei es wie –, 172
Industrie, 15
Inhalt(sangabe), 32, 35
Instrument, 17
interessieren, 3, 119
inzwischen, 158

Jahr, 153
Jahrhundert, 149, 150, 151, 152, 154
jahrhundertelang, 37
Jahrhundertwende, 149
Jahrzehnt, 6, 150
jedenfalls, 69, 78
jetzt, bis –, 163
jüngst, in –er Zeit, 6

Karriere, 47
Kategorie, 139
kaum, 3, 62
keinesfalls, 70
Kenntnis(se), 19
kennzeichnen, 122
klar, 58, 59
    im Klaren sein, 31
    Folgendes wird –, 68
Klasse, 18, 139
klingen, 83
kommen, zum Schluss –, 168
konstruiert, 17
Kontrast, 137, 138, 147
konzentrieren, 53
Krieg, 153
Küchengerät, 17
kühn, 28
Kultur, 15
Kunst, 15, 147
Kurort, 13
kurz, 43, 106
    in aller Kürze, 106
Kurzfassung, 32

Lage, in die - versetzen, 124
lang, vor nicht zu langer Zeit 156
lassen, es lässt sich sagen, 118
Lauf, im –e der Zeit, 161
Laufbahn, 47
Leben, 4, 47
lebenswichtig, 23
legen, Wert – auf, 95
Legende, 36
leiden unter, 141
leider, 100
Leistung, 16
lenken, Aufmerksamkeit – auf, 29, 44
lesen, 28
    beim ersten Lesen, 68
letzte, –n Endes, 162
    in –r Zeit, 6
leugnen, 62, 63
Liebe, 146
liefern, 85
liegen, 14
Linie, in erster –, 22, 32, 35,86
Literatur, 15
lohnen, sich –, 119
lösen, 9, 142
loswerden, 143

machen, 124, 127
mag, es – sein, dass, 97
    das – eine Möglichkeit sein, 175
Maschine, 17
Maß, 115
Meilenstein, 16
Meine Damen und Herren, 1
meinen mit, 30
meinerseits, 71
Meinung, 3, 71, 72
Meinungsverschiedenheiten, 87
Meister, 147
meistern, 142
Meisterwerk, 145
Merkmal, 47
messen, sich – können mit, 131
Methode, 16, 18, 134
Mitte, 149
Mittel, 18
mittlerweile, 158
modern, 11
möglich, 124, 173
Möglichkeit, 175
Musik, 15
mutig, 28

nachdenken, 68
Nachdruck, 95
    mit –, 166
Nachfrage, 132
nachher, 162
Nachkriegszeit, 153
Nachteil, 141, 168
nachweisen, 9, 38, 171
Name, 55, 148
    im Namen, 1
natürlich, 51, 58
Naturschönheit, 13
Nebenhandlung, 35
neigen zu, 5, 68
nennen, 8, 104

Neuerung, 12
neulich, 6, 156
Notfall, 11, 4
nötig, 93, 124
Notiz, 42, 43
notwendig, 93
– machen, 124
Notwendigkeit, 25, 63, 128, 132
nützlich, 130

oben, 38
offen (gesagt), 79
offenbar, 58, 59, 61
offenkundig, 58, 59, 61
offensichtlich, 58, 59, 61
oft, 116, 133
ordnen, 139
Ort, 13

Periode, 35, 150, 153
Person, ich für meine –, 71
politisch, 15
praktisch, 130
Privileg, 1
Problem, 43, 85, 142
proportional, direkt –, 136
verkehrt –, 137

Rang, 10
Redeübung, 32, 171
reduzieren, 126, 127
Regel, 52
Regierung, 155
rein, 86
religiös, 15
Resultat, 6
richtig, 167
Richtung (Tendenz), 5
Rolle, 23

Sache, der – auf den Grund gehen, 68
sagen, 36, 38, 41, 55, 62, 166,167
dasselbe kann man von –, 118
wie der Name schon sagt, 55
schade, 101
schaffen, 96
Schattenseite, 141
schätzen, 11
schauen, genauer –, 68
scheinen, 60, 68, 72, 78, 83, 97
schlechter machen, 124
schließen, 74, 168
schließlich, 92, 96, 162, 167
schlimmste, im –n Falle, 114
Schluss 162, 166, 169
zum – kommen, 168
Schlüssel, 85
Schritt, 12
Schul–, 15
schwer, schwierig, 3, 79
Schwierigkeit, 1, 42
sehen, 38
so haben wir gesehen, dass, 169
Sehenswürdigkeit, 13
selbe, das–, 136
selbstverständlich, 37, 58, 59, 62
seltsam, 28, 78
sicher, 56, 167
eines ist –, 172
– wissen, 67
Sicherheit, mit – sagen können, 167
sichern, 124
Sinn, 102, 103, 104
so, 169
so genannt, 104
soll (angeblich), 75
sonderbar, 28, 78
sorgen für, 144
Sorgfalt, 95
sorgfältig, 68
Sorte, 18
sozusagen, 105
spannend, 28
später, 38, 162
spiegeln, 145, 146
spielen, eine Rolle –, 23
Sport, 15
sprechen, für etwas –, 90
Sprichwort, 36
Stadt, 13
Standpunkt, 31, 113
steigend, 115, 132
steigern, 125, 127
Stellung, 10
stoßen auf, 28, 142
Strömung (Tendenz), 5
Studium, 68

Tag, 155
14 Tage, 156
Tagung, 1
Tat, in der –, 66, 82
Tatsache, 66, 85
tatsächlich, 66, 82
Technik (Wissenschaft), 16
(Verfahren), 134
technisch, 16
Teil, 139
teilweise, 84
Tendenz 5
Thema, 31, 33, 46
Titel, 55, 139
Tradition, 36
tun, 127, 129
zu – haben mit, 142
Type, 18, 141
typisch, 11, 121

überbewerten, 94
Überblick, 32
überlegen, 26, 29, 31, 119, 167, 168
Überlegung, 31, 68, 95
überprüfen, 44
Überprüfung, 68
überraschend, 58, 120
überschätzen, 94
Überschrift, 55, 139
übersehen, 94

Übersicht, 32
übertragener Sinn, 103
übertreiben, 94
überwinden, 142
überzeugt, 3, 56, 78
üblich, 116
übrigens, 40
umfassen, 35, 140
umgekehrt, 82
– proportional, 137
umhin, ich kann nicht – zu, 77
Umstand, 108, 109, 110, 166
um zu, 127
unbedingt, 93
unbekannt, 66
unberücksichtigt, 51
unerlässlich, 93
unerreicht, 131
ungefähr, 102, 136
ungewöhnlich, 28
unglaublich, 120
unglaubwürdig, 83, 120
unglücklich, 101
unglücklicherweise, 100
ungünstig, 131
unlängst, 6, 156
unleugbar, 62
unmittelbar, 153
unmöglich, 98, 124
unnötig, 124
unschätzbar, 17
unsicher, 65
Unsicherheit, 65
unten, 38
unter anderem, 48
unternehmen, Anstrengungen –, 6
unterschätzen, 94
unterscheiden, 137, 138
Unterschied, 135, 138
unterstreichen, 25, 166
untersuchen, 44
Untersuchung, 68
unterteilen, 139
untrennbar, 21
unübertroffen, 131
unvereinbar, 89
unvergleichlich, 131
unvermeidlicherweise, 96
unvorhersagbar, 172
unvorstellbar, 4
unwahrscheinlich, 60
unweigerlich, 96
Urlaubsort 11, 13
ursprünglich, 103
urteilen, 26, 74

Veränderung, 6
Veranstaltung, 15
verbessern, 124
Verbesserung, 6, 12
Verbindung, 21
verblüffend, 28, 120
verbreitet, 17, 133
verbunden, 21
verdanken, 19
vereinfachen, 124
Verfahren, 18, 134
Verfügung, zur – stehen, 144
Vergangenheit, 155
vergegenwärtigen, sich – 31, 119
vergessen, 40
vergleichen, 131, 147
vergleichsweise, 48, 102
Vergnügen, 1
vergrößern, 125, 127
Verhältnisse, 166
verhindern, 126
verkehrt proportional, 137
vermehren, 125, 127
vermeiden, 126
vermindern, 126, 127
vermuten, 37, 73, 74
vermutlich, 59, 73
vernachlässigen, 94
Versammlung, 1
verschieden, 18, 137
Verschiedenheit, 135
verstehen, 26
– unter, 30
es versteht sich von selbst, 62
Versuch, 7
vertraut, 20, 26
sich – machen, 26
verursachen, 96, 128
verwandtes Gebiet, 133
verweisen auf, 38, 39, 41, 48
verwenden, verwerten, 17, 133, 134
Verwendung, 103
verwerfen, 134
vielseitig, 11
vor allem, 48
vorbringen, 37
Vordergrund, in den – treten, 24
vorhanden, 144
vorher, 38, 44, 155, 165
Vorkriegszeit, 153
Vorlesung, 32
Vorliebe, 146
Vorrecht, 1
Vorrichtung, 17
vorstellen, sich –, 1, 3, 4, 79
Vorstellung (Idee), 26, 29
Vorteil, 141, 168
Vortrag, 32, 171
Vorzug, 141, 146, 168

wachsend, 115, 132
wagemutig, 28
wahr, 82, 83, 97
Wahrheit, 78
wahrscheinlich, 59, 60, 84
Wahrscheinlichkeit, 59
Wahrzeichen, 16
walten, Sorgfalt – lassen, 95
wegdenken, sich aus dem Leben –, 4
Weile, 162
Weise, auf diese –, 173
weiterer, 42, 43
im weitesten Sinne, 102

weit verbreitet, 17, 133
Weltkrieg, 153
Wendepunkt, 16
wenig denken an, 3
Werk, 145, 146, 1, 47
Wert, 17, 95
wertschätzen, 11, 25, 26
wertvoll, 12, 17, 129, 130
wesentlich, 11, 23, 91, 92, 123, 135
    im Wesentlichen, 22
wichtig, 11, 15, 16, 23, 91, 92, 129, 135
Wichtigkeit, 25, 91, 94
widerspiegeln, 145, 1, 46
wiederholen, 166
willkommen heißen, 1
Wirkung, 123
wirtschaftlich, 15
wissen, 26, 57, 172
    – wollen, 67
wissenschaftlich, 15
Woche, 156
Wort, 118
    – ergreifen, 1
    mit einem –, 106
    mit anderen Worten, 107
wörtlich, 103
Wurzel, 68

zählen zu, 11, 15, 140
zahlreich, 18
zeigen, 9, 38, 145, 146
Zeit, im Laufe der –, 161
    in letzter –, 6
    in unserer –, 154, 155
    von – zu –, 159
    vor dieser –, 165
    vor nicht zu langer –, 156
    zu seiner –, 155
Zeitalter, 2, 150
Zeitschrift, 27, 35
Zeitspanne, 35, 150, 153
Zeitungsbericht, 27
Zentrum, 15
Ziel, 34, 127
Zielsetzung, 127
zitieren, 48
zögern, 79
zollen, Anerkennung –, 174
zugeben, 62, 76
Zukunft, 172, 175
zuletzt, 162
zunächst, zuerst, 29, 30, 141, 162
zurückgehen (zurückreichen) in, 151
zurückkommen auf, 44
zurückverfolgen bis, 151
zurückzuführen auf, 19, 84
zusammenfassen, 139, 166
Zusammenfassung, 32
Zusammenhang, 21, 29
zusammensetzen, 22
zuschreiben, 19, 84
zustimmen, 56
zuträglich, 130
zutreffen, 80, 81, 82
zuwenden, sich –, 44, 45
Zweck, 17, 34, 110, 127
zwecklos, 98
Zweifel, 63
zweifelhaft, 65
zweifellos, 64